Cooking through Treatment *to* Recovery

Easy, Flavorful Recipes to Prevent and Decrease Side Effects at Every Stage of Conventional Therapy

Lisa A. Price, ND, and Susan Gins, MA, MS, CN

Photographs by Stewart Hopkins
Food styling by Nancy Werner

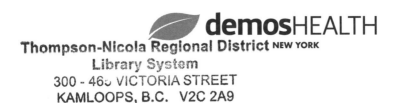

demosHEALTH NEW YORK

Visit our website at www.demoshealth.com

ISBN: 978-1-936303-80-9 (paperback)
ISBN: 978-1-936303-82-3 (hardcover)
e-book ISBN: 978-1-61705-238-5

Acquisitions Editor: Julia Pastore
Compositor: DiacriTech

Medical information provided by Demos Health, in the absence of a visit with a health-care professional, must be considered as an educational service only. This book is not designed to replace a physician's independent judgment about the appropriateness or risks of a procedure or therapy for a given patient. Our purpose is to provide you with information that will help you make your own health-care decisions.

The information and opinions provided here are believed to be accurate and sound, based on the best judgment available to the authors, editors, and publisher, but readers who fail to consult appropriate health authorities assume the risk of injuries. The publisher is not responsible for errors or omissions. The editors and publisher welcome any reader to report to the publisher any discrepancies or inaccuracies noticed.

Library of Congress Cataloging-in-Publication Data
Price, Lisa A.
    Cooking through cancer treatment to recovery : easy, flavorful recipes to prevent and decrease side effects at every stage of conventional therapy / Lisa A. Price, ND, and Susan Gins, MA, MS, CN; photographs by Stewart Hopkins; food styling by Nancy Werner.
        pages cm
    Includes bibliographical references and index.
    ISBN 978-1-936303-80-9 — ISBN 978-1-936303-82-3 — ISBN 978-1-61705-238-5
    1. Cancer—Diet therapy—Recipes. I. Gins, Susan. II. Hopkins, Stewart. III. Werner, Nancy. IV. Title.
    RC271.D52P736 2015
    641.5′631—dc23
                              2014042962

Special discounts on bulk quantities of Demos Health books are available to corporations, professional associations, pharmaceutical companies, health-care organizations, and other qualifying groups. For details, please contact:

Special Sales Department
Demos Medical Publishing, LLC
11 West 42nd Street, 15th Floor
New York, NY 10036
Phone: 800-532-8663 or 212-683-0072
Fax: 212-941-7842
E-mail: specialsales@demosmedical.com

Printed in the United States of America by McNaughton & Gunn.

15 16 17 18 19 / 5 4 3 2

Lisa A. Price: To Eloise Wilson and to all people diagnosed with cancer.

Susan Gins: To my husband, Stephen Gins, whose ongoing encouragement, intelligence, and love supported me on this journey, and to my patients, who validated that changing one's food is changing one's life.

Contents

Hope is a thing with feathers that perches in the soul.

—Emily Dickinson

INTRODUCTION

Discover how food can help you get through cancer treatment successfully. Choosing the right nutrients at this time will bring you closer to wellness and give you a sense of independence and peace of mind.

This book contains resources and recipes you need to get through these next several months of treatment with minimal side effects. For some, this information will simply be a reorganization of what you already know about healthy eating. For others, the information will be very new. Luckily, our book serves as a complete hassle-free guide. It includes descriptions of symptoms you may experience at each step of cancer treatment, what foods are most helpful, and why. The Quick Glance Chart on pages 121–129 will help you quickly find recipes for your stage of treatment and side effects. We provide suggestions for stocking your pantry with healthy ingredients. We also list cancer support groups and major scientific studies documenting the effects of food on cancer development and recovery.

The more than 100 recipes in this book, while maintaining delicious flavor and aesthetic appeal, contain targeted nutrients. They are low in saturated fats, with no soy, dairy, gluten, or processed sugar; according to the Food and Drug Administration, these foods are more likely to cause inflammation and inflammatory damage to the body. They are best avoided.

With so much information on the Internet it is difficult to know what foods and meals are the most healthful and appropriate during different phases of cancer treatment. As a result of many requests from patients, caretakers, friends, and families who seek ways to help, we've written this cookbook.

Typically, patients seek out our services for advice on supplements and nutrition. Many assume that an "anticancer" diet will be tasteless, unappetizing, and will include nothing fun or comforting. In fact, a question we're asked at least once a week in our complementary cancer care practice is:

"I don't have to give up chocolate, do I, doctor?"

There is a sigh of relief when the answer is no.

And we usually follow with, "But chocolate will not be enough. You'll have to rely on a sound, healthful diet to help get you through treatment with minimal side effects."

However, healing food does not have to taste awful or be absent of comforting affects. And that's good, because who wants to eat cardboard-like biscuits at a time like this? Most patients find the dietary changes to be a wonderful discovery of new flavors that provide the added benefit of achieving optimal health through cancer treatment and beyond.

A cancer diagnosis is one of the single most traumatic events you can experience. It can throw your life into a state of chaos. Due to the loss of control, the overriding emotion involves shock and fear. This can turn your life upside down and numb you.

Conventional treatment often happens quickly, before your emotional state can catch up. A whirlwind flurry of doctor's appointments and anticipation of test results begins. You trust in competent health care providers, yet there is so much information you don't know where to begin. What a state and lifestyle change! Especially if you have been self-sufficient and independent most of your life.

In the meantime, friends and loved ones search for ways to say "I am here and I am on your side." At this point your yearnings for chocolate and comfort foods may be stronger than ever. Unfortunately, chocolate's nutrient value and effects are limited, only carrying you so far through the hills and valleys of cancer and cancer treatment.

What are we to do when we receive a diagnosis of cancer? What choices can we make to empower ourselves during this overwhelming period of time? The good news is that there is an abundance of whole foods that can successfully get you through cancer treatment. Whole foods provide nutrients that can be powerful tools to work alongside surgery, radiation, chemotherapy, and hormone therapy. Food choices can affect outcomes of therapies, help to decrease interruptions in treatments, promote healing, decrease risk of infection, and increase quality of life. Becoming informed and making choices about food can be the place where you find a sense of control and empowerment during cancer treatment.

Nutrition can help make your recovery successful by addressing specific health needs. Importantly, your immune system and metabolism need to be working optimally to destroy cancer cells and deal with the side effects of conventional therapy. Food can also stabilize mood, and staying optimistic and hopeful is key to improving immune activity and outcome.

We use food as a primary complementary therapy in our private naturopathic and nutrition practices. More often than not, cancer patients want daily menu plans. They want guidelines for daily carbohydrate, protein, fat, and fiber that will benefit them, specifically when going through treatment. They seek recipes that are quick, easy, and wholesome, yet tasty. Recipes not laden with fats and sugar that may increase side effects rather than decrease them. They want a guide as to which nutrients are helpful during specific treatments and what foods aid in absorption and digestion. They also seek recipes that can feed the whole family, promoting health and prevention for loved ones as well. Caretakers, friends, and families seek ways to help the patients, and most want to contribute by preparing meals.

To meet these needs, we have designed a user-friendly cookbook organized by meal, course, and treatment. We have balanced the major food groups based on specific nutrient needs during different phases and types of conventional therapy, and our recipes are based on alleviating general symptoms that occur during each of these therapies (i.e., surgery, radiation, chemotherapy, and hormone treatment). Using a complement of three daily meals and supplemental snacks from our cookbook will provide complete protein, carbohydrate, and fat needs, as well as the nutrients that are most beneficial for each phase of cancer treatment. This is a one stop cookbook for patients, friends, and family, containing recipes that are full of health and inspiration.

A beauty emerges as many cancer patients base their choices on self-care and self-compassion. There is an attention to life and detail that emerges. As one of my patients responded to a general question:

"My husband and I have begun to look at things with a child's eyes. We stop to look at the very small things that, before cancer, I would have called insignificant—like a colony of ants moving crumbs to their nest. If I didn't have cancer, I wouldn't take time to just watch."

Often, relationships resolve, change, and strengthen as we focus on them more directly. Optimal life becomes the goal. This includes choices about what goes in and on your body.

In this walk through what seems like a valley in your life, remember, there are flowers growing in the valleys. Look for the best choices for yourself, and receive the gifts that are offered. Use hope and the healing power of food as your allies to motivate you toward greater wellness and optimal health.

Be inspired to be well!

My relationship to living changed. A person diagnosed with cancer is regularly inundated with imagery of battles and fighting, and admonished to create a strong will to survive. All of these things equate living with success, and living happening when the cancer is beaten. My strategy was this: Radical acceptance. To experience everything with an open heart. Yes, everything. This evolved into the awareness that cancer isn't a fight, it's a surrender. The more adept I became at giving up and letting go, the more room I made for the joy and peace I was having now. *Ultimately, our destination is death, but until that moment we are alive. Live.*

—*Brandi Chase*

FOOD AS MEDICINE

Food, glorious food! Foods come in every color of the rainbow and provide a cornucopia of beauty. Food brings us together daily and for special occasions. Its aromas can stimulate our appetites and perhaps take us back to significant points in our lives. Every culture on earth has daily meal rituals and customary foods that are important to communing.

Food can serve as medicine too. It provides nutrients involved in healing. In fact, food is probably the most commonly consumed "drug" available to all without a prescription. Certain foods can act as anti-inflammatory agents, antidepressants, diuretics, digestives, antibiotics, and anticoagulants, without the side effects that so commonly accompany conventional drugs. Except in cases of allergic reactions, food is rarely harmful.

However, the Standard American Diet is deficient in a number of nutrients, including fiber, magnesium, potassium, and calcium. These nutrients are involved in several important processes in our bodies, and lacking them can result in diseases such as hypertension, constipation, heart palpitations, fatigue, insomnia, osteopenia, and osteoporosis. During conventional cancer treatment, you need these nutrients even more, because they also repair and restore damaged tissues. You can address deficiencies with the selective intake of food.

Specific foods can be used successfully to decrease symptoms and improve quality of life during conventional cancer treatments without decreasing the effects of surgery, radiation, chemotherapy, or hormone therapy. Many foods contain antioxidants and other nutrients such as folate. If these nutrients were given as supplements they could potentially interfere with the effectiveness of, say, chemotherapy and radiation. But because foods only contain small dosages of these nutrients—unless we overindulge—we do not have to worry about this. They provide enough to help keep the normal tissues healthy and the immune system active, but not enough to interfere with the effectiveness of the conventional drug.

For Every Stage of Cancer Therapy

Importance of Protein

Of all nutrients, protein is one of the most essential during cancer treatment. Protein is found in every cell of our body and plays many important roles in cellular function. Chemotherapy and radiation destroy cancer cells, but they can affect healthy cells as well, depleting protein in the process and increasing our protein needs. Dead cells need to be replaced and damaged cells need to be repaired. This high turnover of protein can create a shortage of the amino acids that are the building blocks needed to replace and repair tissues, neurotransmitters, and hormones.

Protein also provides direct fuel for immune, gut, and kidney cells, all of which tend to be depressed by chemotherapy, radiation, and prolonged stress.

Protein is needed for proper metabolism, and when we find ourselves short of this nutrient we are more prone to developing fatigue, foggy memory, sleep problems, and anemia, among other issues. Proper protein absorption from the gut also allows adequate water absorption to take place, allowing better overall hydration. Being hydrated through chemotherapy and radiation is extremely important to long- and short-term recovery.

We recommend that your diet be heavy on plant-based protein and fish, with red meat restricted to three times a week or less. Scientific studies have shown that red and processed meats increase colorectal cancer risk and inflammation whereas intake of fish decreases these risks.

Protein needs when not undergoing cancer treatment is calculated by:

1. Taking your weight in pounds and dividing by 2.2 (which is your weight in kilograms).
2. Taking that number and multiplying by 0.8.
3. The result gives the grams of protein normally needed daily.

During cancer treatment, this will be the *minimum* amount of protein you will need daily. And it is important to spread the protein out during the day, including it in all meals and snacks. This will help keep your energy level stable. You can eat more plant-based protein and eggs if you want.

In general, approximately 50 to 80 grams of protein from your diet is needed while going through treatment, but you should always check with your health care provider for your specific requirements. People with conditions such as diabetes and kidney disease may have different requirements.

Recipes in this book, particularly those for breakfast, lunch, and dinner, contain adequate amounts of protein and, in combination with other daily meals, meet the requirements given above. Each recipe in this book lists its provided amount of protein in grams near the top of the page. Rest assured that each recipe is planned to complement our daily recommendation for protein and other nutrients we discuss.

For cancer prevention and throughout treatment, adequate amounts of protein are important in maintaining proper blood glucose levels. Why is your blood sugar level so important? For over 30 years the association between diabetes type 2 and increased cancer risk has been known (there seems to be no association between diabetes type 1 and cancer). In diabetes type 2 we find an insulin-resistant condition. In other words, insulin secretion is high and glucose levels are high because the glucose can't get into the cells. So, is the problem the glucose? Is this "feeding" the cancer? Well, based on emerging research the answer is not so simple. It appears the insulin is the culprit. High insulin levels, the kind found in prediabetics and people with diabetes type 2, is associated with a higher risk for developing certain types of cancers. The take-home message is that your best bet is to maintain proper levels of blood glucose so as not to give cancer an advantage. This is where protein comes into play as a fuel that provides long-term energy stores, helping to maintain energy levels and proper blood glucose levels.

Carbohydrates

Carbohydrates are the body's main source of quick energy. Most ingested carbohydrates are used as fuel, and the rest are stored as fat. There are two categories of carbohydrates: simple and complex. The two primarily differ in fiber and nutrient content.

Simple carbohydrates come from fruits, sweeteners, and processed grains. Fruits provide nutrients that help the body fight disease and infection, and usually only a smaller amount of fiber compared to vegetables. Refined products such as white bread, cookies, and cakes mainly serve as quick fuel, even when they may be fortified with vitamins and minerals. The American Heart Association recommends no more than 25 grams of simple carbohydrates per day for women and 35 grams per day for men.

The best carbohydrates are complex. And the best sources of these include vegetables and whole grains, which also supply vitamins, minerals, fiber, and phytonutrients to the body's cells and contain both soluble and insoluble fiber. Soluble fiber is important to helping maintain proper gut flora, which may be disrupted by ingestion of antibiotics or pain medication. Insoluble fiber helps bulking in the colon and thus proper formation of stool. Based on findings from the European Prospective Investigation into Cancer and Nutrition (EPIC) study, diets high in fiber reduce colorectal cancer risk. Fiber is protective.

Both types of fiber are helpful for healing the digestive tract as well as helping with the elimination of toxins, including hormones and drugs. Fiber also slows down the absorption of carbohydrates, and this means you feel fuller longer and are less likely to overeat—which can happen if you are on steroids during chemotherapy. Fiber also helps decrease nausea and constipation, and it is beneficial for a healthy cardiovascular system and proper blood pressure levels.

It's recommended that a balanced diet include 20 to 35 grams of dietary fiber per day. Our recipes contain almost all complex carbohydrates and meet or exceed these daily recommended fiber levels. However, some people will need to alter their daily fiber intake. This applies to people who have undergone gastrointestinal surgeries such as those for colon and rectal cancers. We've noted recipes that should be avoided if you are on a low-fiber diet.

Good Fats

Fats are a vital building block in our bodies. They are important in storage of fuel, making hormones, blood clotting, managing inflammation, and providing insulation for body temperature. They are integral to cell membranes and keep our skin healthy. Dietary fat helps absorb the fat-soluble vitamins A, E, D, and K, and even some fat-soluble antioxidants from vegetables. All of these vitamins are important in normal growth, development, and proper immune function. For example, vitamin D deficiency has a correlation to increased risk of cancer. People living in the northern hemisphere have a tendency to be deficient due to the angle of the sun not activating vitamin D in the skin sufficiently. The USDA dietary guidelines recommend adults consume about 20% to 30% of their calories from fats. The Standard American Diet contains about 34% to 40%.

Like carbohydrates, there are two categories of fats: saturated and unsaturated. Saturated fats come mostly from animal products. These should be limited.

Unsaturated fats come mostly from vegetable oils and nuts. These fats have been shown to lower cholesterol and cardiovascular disease.

Unsaturated fats contain omega-3 fatty acids that are particularly important during cancer treatment and in prevention. Although they provide no anti-oxidant properties, they have anti-inflammatory capabilities. The dietary intake for unsaturated fats should be 65 to 70 grams. Our recipes contain a complement of good fats and the daily recommended intake. The exact amounts are listed on each recipe.

Counting Nutrients

During cancer treatment the goal is to maintain a stable weight, and replenish healthful amounts of nutrients that help to regenerate damaged tissues. The focus should move from counting calories to counting nutrients. There are common, specific foods that contain particular targeted nutrients that are helpful in reducing or preventing side effects. For example, oysters and leafy greens such as kale contain good amounts of magnesium, which, when deficient, can cause a number of conditions, including constipation, muscle cramping, and hypertension. We provide an index of common foods found in our recipes and the nutrients they contain. This should help you choose foods rich in the nutrients you need most, select from our recipes, and create your own. We've also identified recipes that are high in certain key nutrients (providing over 10% of the daily value) or are a good source of them (providing at least 10%).

For Specific Stages of Cancer Therapy

In the last several years, conventional therapy has moved from simply prolonging cancer patients' lives to actually saving them. Conventional therapies, which are constantly changing according to developments in science and in technology, aim to locate, locally remove, and reduce the number of tumor cells. These therapies are vital to the survival of most patients, but they have side effects and long-term potential health risks, and each therapy increases the need for specific dietary nutrients. Let's take a brief look at these therapies and how nutrition can play a role in decreasing side effects.

Surgery

Surgery is the oldest method used to treat cancer and offers the greatest chance for a cure. Different cancer types require different surgery.

Types of surgery include:

1. Curative surgery is recommended when cancer cells are localized and may be removed almost entirely by surgery.

2. Debulking surgery removes only part of a tumor, leaving radiation or chemotherapy to kill the remaining cells.

3. Diagnostic and staging surgeries help your doctor evaluate how far cancer cells have spread.

Patients' physical health and nutritional status can affect the outcome and the side effects after surgery. Patients deficient in zinc and vitamin E, for example, may take longer to heal.

Pain at the site of surgery is the most common side effect. To treat pain, patients are often given medication that results in constipation. This slow bowel activity can sometimes become a very serious problem of gastrointestinal blockage. If the blockage is severe, surgery will be required and will often require the removal of a section of the bowel. Side effects of this surgery can be diarrhea, constipation, or both. Surgery can also pose a risk of infection, which would require treatment with antibiotics.

You can select nutrition prior to and after surgery that will enable you to recover quicker, decrease the need for or frequency of antibiotics, and help to restore proper bowel function.

Before surgery you should opt for a diet rich in nutrients. As a reminder, nutrients are minerals such as calcium and magnesium, and vitamins such as folate and thiamine, which your body needs to properly function. Nutrients also include the three major food groups: proteins, complex carbohydrates, and good fats.

Your diet should include plenty of both raw and cooked vegetables, plenty of protein, and plenty of whole grains containing fiber. Broths and soups packed with nutrients will help with anxiety and insomnia. Being well-hydrated will help you tolerate and recover from anesthesia.

Pineapple and papaya are two fruits that contain digestive enzymes. These are helpful for reducing inflammation and for decreasing scarring. Melons, nectarines, and other fruits high in soluble fiber can help in keeping the bowels moving after surgery. Foods high in vitamin D, the sunshine vitamin, will help skin repair and immunity. Foods containing good amounts of vitamin D include cold-water fish.

Recipe recommendations include berries high in phytonutrient content, broths with mushrooms, the high antioxidant–containing spice turmeric, and the antimicrobial spice garlic. Foods in our recipes identified for surgery are selected for their vitamin E, C, and D levels as well as a high fiber content to help prevent constipation. A particular focus is placed on protein, which will be needed to repair and restore tissues. Our salad and vegetable selections contain bitters that will help to stimulate digestive juices, another way to help with digestion and elimination.

Chemotherapy

Chemotherapy is a chemical agent or drug administered to the body in order to destroy the cancer cells that linger after surgery. It also may be administered before surgery as what is called neoadjuvant therapy, to shrink the size of the tumor. Treatment usually consists of a combination of therapies. For example, docetaxel and cyclophosphomide may be used together, or a combination of 5-fluorouracil and methotrexate. Chemotherapy can be taken orally or it may be infused or injected. It is administered over time, usually in cycles of once a week or once every two to three weeks, depending on the therapy, type, and stage of the cancer. Chemotherapy is often administered with steroids to decrease the chance of an allergic reaction. Patients are often also given antacids and antinausea drugs. Sometimes they may still be on pain medications or antibiotics from surgery.

Different chemotherapies work in different ways. Some work to generate free radicals that aim to damage the DNA of the rapidly dividing tumor cells. Some work by mimicking natural factors needed to make DNA. Others work by preventing cell division, growth, and the cell's ability to make energy.

However, chemotherapy is not selective between cancer cells and normally dividing cells. This is why most of the side effects happen. All cells that replicate are affected: hair, nails, bone marrow, and cells in the digestive tract.

Interestingly enough, patients experience most of the side effects most strongly at three to four days after administration of the drugs. With each cycle the side effects tend to be more noticeable. Being well-rested with eight hours or more of sleep, well-hydrated with 64 ounces or more of clear water, and well-nourished, all seem to be a great help with side effects and your ability to rebound.

Chemotherapy can take an incredible toll, both physically and emotionally. Common side effects of chemotherapy and the drugs that are often administered with them include anemia, brain fog, indigestion or acid reflux, stomach upset and gas, mouth sores, constipation, fatigue, nausea, loss of appetite, loss or alteration of taste, peripheral neuropathy, and anal irritation. These symptoms are associated with the type of chemotherapy given.

Nutrient focus during chemotherapy should aim to aid digestion and absorption and decrease acid reflux. Addressing these will serve to decrease most of the side effects mentioned earlier. Tasty meals containing complex carbohydrates and a protein complement are helpful. Foods with adequate B vitamins, magnesium, zinc, and calcium top the list as well.

It's recommended that foods be cooked or steamed lightly, not raw. Raw foods pose increased risk of infection because sometimes the immune system has been lowered as a result of chemotherapy. Ability to digest is often lowered during chemotherapy. Cooking food helps to break down fiber and aid your body's digestive ability. Bitters (such as collard greens and arugula), foods high in glutamine (such as eggs), and foods high in electrolytes (such as broths), are a good bet during this time. Calcium and tryptophan/glycine-containing foods, for example turkey and kale, help to induce sleep and prevent insomnia and anxiety, and in turn help to avoid depression of the immune system.

Sometimes chemotherapy causes low red blood cell counts (anemia) or low white blood cell counts (leukopenia). Foods such as apricots and molasses, high in iron, can help build the blood back up. Fish is an excellent protein source at this time because of its omega-3 fatty acid content; it reduces inflammation and also contains vitamin D. During chemotherapy, try to avoid eating raw cruciferous vegetables such as broccoli and cabbage. They are very high in nutrients but can produce a lot of gas and gastrointestinal discomfort. Reducing beans (unless soaked to decrease gas) is also helpful—we use lentils and split peas instead. Asparagus, if it's in season, is a sure bet, given its culinary dose of glutathione.

Chemotherapy can also cause a disruption in taste sensation for many people. Strong-tasting foods can help with this problem. The use of salt, sweeteners, and even some condiments such as mustard can help improve food's taste. As mentioned earlier, foods containing magnesium, copper, and zinc are helpful for maintaining and restoring taste. Foods high in these nutrients include nuts, kale, collards, and cilantro.

Radiation

Radiation uses high-energy x-rays to destroy rapidly growing cancer cells. It is recommended for all kinds of solid tumors. The goal of radiation is to eliminate an entire tumor while it still occupies a confined space, or radiate an area where a tumor once occupied a space. About half of the people diagnosed with cancer undergo radiation as part of their treatment process.

A common side effect is skin irritation at the site of treatment. Radiation can cause permanent discoloration or scarring in certain patients, and sometimes hair loss at the site of treatment.

Some patients battle fatigue, which affects the patient's ability to remain active and alert throughout the day. If lymph nodes are irradiated, swelling, also known as lymphedema, can result; this condition involves fluid retention in the limbs and needs medical attention.

Foods containing adequate protein, electrolytes, good fats, micronutrients (minerals that our body requires in small amounts, but are vital to health), minerals, vitamin E, and omega-3 fatty acids can help. If white blood cell counts have returned to normal, patients may begin to eat raw foods again. This can provide quite a boost in energy and also in mood. Foods high in vitamin C such as berries and Brussels sprouts can also be useful as long as they are not overconsumed. Pineapple, papaya, and avocado can reduce scarring and promote healing. Broths and asparagus help to restore healthful immune cells and boost energy.

Hormone Therapy

Hormone therapy prevents cancer cells from using hormones like estrogen and testosterone, which they need to grow and divide. This treatment, used for certain types of breast and prostate cancers, may include the use of drugs that stop the production of certain hormones or that change the way hormones are made.

Hormones serve a very important function in the body. For example, estrogen protects against bone loss and is slightly anti-inflammatory. Estrogen prevents calcium from leaking out of bone tissue and therefore helps to keep the body strong. Testosterone serves to maintain muscle mass. Their withdrawal from the system can result in some short- and long-term side effects such as increased risk of blood clotting, changes in appetite, fluid retention, hot flashes and night sweats, tiredness, weight gain, and muscle and joint pain.

During hormone therapy, we can start reintroducing fresh fruits and salads because, in most cases, digestive complaints and issues with low white blood cell counts have been resolved.

During this period of time we are wise to be careful with phytoestrogenic foods and caffeine. Phytoestrogens are naturally occurring chemicals in plants that can act like our own estrogens with certain types of cancers. They are contained in a number of foods but occur at highest concentrations in soy and tofu products. Research has shown that foods containing phytoestrogens and other hormone mimics from plants can have both positive and negative effects on cancer.

Foods high in calcium and micronutrients, such as magnesium, boron, and manganese, combat estrogen withdrawal symptoms such as bone loss, hot flashes, night sweats, joint aches, and osteoporosis. Foods high in omega-3 fatty acids also help with hormonal withdrawal symptoms.

Withdrawal of hormones can also result in decreased stamina and fatigue. Recipes high in protein, low in simple sugars, and moderate in whole grains help in recapturing stamina and building muscle mass. Foods high in antioxidants such as CoQ10, turmeric, garlic, and rosemary repair damage from chemotherapy and radiation. They will also begin to build your body's defenses against developing cancer again.

High nutrient content and moderate calorie-containing foods will combat weight gain from steroids in chemotherapy. Foods containing vitamins B and C can combat adrenal disturbances from mental and physical trauma.

Recovery and Prevention

While recovering from treatment, focus on foods that increase energy and stamina, build muscles, and maintain bone mass. Bone mass maintenance will be particularly important for patients on hormone therapy. During this period of time it will also be imperative to eat foods that promote good sleep, optimal bowel function, and absorption. Our recipes identified for this phase are specially designed to meet these goals.

With most conventional drugs and their potential side effects out of the way, we can begin to introduce a wider array of foods and preparations, as well as spices.

Some nutrients particularly helpful during recovery and prevention will include foods and spices such as broccoli, turmeric, and garlic, which are high in micronutrients such as magnesium, calcium, manganese, and selenium as well as rich sources of vitamins A, C, and E and bioactive constituents that have been shown to have anticancer effects.

Additional Therapies Supporting Conventional Treatment

You may also be using some alternative, also known as complementary, therapies during conventional treatment. Complementary therapies are rational, evidence-based practices, delivered or taught by trained and licensed practitioners such as naturopathic physicians and integrative oncologists. They are often used by cancer patients in concert or synergy with conventional medicine and conventional cancer treatment. These therapies may include lifestyle counseling, nutrition advice, acupuncture, and massage therapy. The objective of all these therapies is to decrease the side effects of conventional treatment while increasing the quality of life for patients. Most importantly, all do this without decreasing the effectiveness of conventional therapies.

A naturopathic physician providing complementary cancer care often works in very close association with the conventional cancer care team. Most have specialized training in their fields, which can include many years of research training in immunology and/or oncology. Because medical doctors are not trained to use specific nutrition and supplement therapies, patients turn to naturopaths for this information. The benefit is a progressive, holistic team approach to health care.

Therapies used by naturopathic doctors depend on the stage and nature of the cancer, the conventional therapy being used, and the symptoms experienced by the patient. Vitamin and mineral supplements, diet, and nutrition are most frequently prescribed, and tend to be very effective. Herbal therapies are less often prescribed because there are often problems with quality control and contamination of the herbs. Some herbals therapies can also pose a risk of undermining conventional treatments. If you do seek a complementary practitioner to work with during conventional treatment, make sure he or she has received proper training, licensing, and accreditations and has established rapport with a medical oncologist.

None of the recommendations in this book should interfere with alternative or complementary therapies, but always discuss changes to your diet with your health care provider.

Final tips for getting through treatment:

■ **Hydration**

Make sure you drink at least 64 ounces (eight glasses) of water starting at least two days before chemotherapy treatment and continuing for at least three days after treatment. Dehydration can lead to exacerbation of nausea and fatigue. If water just doesn't taste right during treatment, you can try to add some lemon juice to your water, or use carbonated water.

■ **Sleep/rest**

We've observed that patients who are well rested bounce back from all treatment phases more quickly. It can be tough to sleep through pain and the steroid treatment. Consult with your health care provider if you need assistance with sleep. It will be worth it.

(continued)

◼ Exercise

According to the EPIC study, the top factor corresponding to positive effects on cancer prevention and remission is exercise. In addition, other positive effects include sustained stamina, energy, bowel regularity, and mood stabilization.

◼ Support

This is a period of time to ask for help and to rely on those family and friends who want to assist. It is hoped that this period of treatment will be a blink of time in your life. Be smart, and don't go through it alone or without asking for help.

In 2004, Dan Buettner, CEO of the Blue Zones Project, partnered with researchers from National Geographic to study the places around the world that enjoy the greatest longevity. They found that what distinguishes places like Ikaria, Greece, and Okinawa, Japan, are environments and cultural attributes that foster community, family life, and physical activity.

I have truly learned to enjoy the little pleasures of life to a significant degree. Never take anything for granted. We are all hanging by a thread and will never know what may befall us in the near future. Spend your time doing what you love or what you absolutely must do. Life is so precious.

—Fern Rogow

HOW TO USE THIS BOOK

This cookbook provides you with recipes that are balanced for the nutrients you need most during specific phases of conventional cancer treatment. The nutrients chosen for each recipe are based on addressing general side effects associated with surgery, radiation, chemotherapy, or hormone therapy. It is designed to provide a complete diet that does not interfere or reduce the effectiveness of conventional treatment. You will notice that most of the recipes are plant based, and do not contain dairy, gluten, or refined sugar. Research shows that a plant-based diet is the best way to maintain disease-free health. We also seek to decrease inflammation and thus have chosen foods with low inflammatory indexes. These are foods that contain nutrients that decrease damage done by inflammation.

We intend to ease you into healthful choices through delicious and nutritious foods, so this cookbook is designed to be used with minimal thought and time. Choosing recipes from breakfast, lunch, snack, and dinner menus will supply you with the recommended dietary intake for protein, carbohydrates, and fats. Most of the recipes take between 15 and, at most, 40 minutes to prepare. The ingredients are usually basic, and all should be easy to find. We include a general shopping list to get your pantry stocked with cancer-fighting ingredients.

Recipes are grouped by meal, and each recipe is coded with several icons, each of which corresponds to a phase of conventional treatment:

Pretreatment/Surgery	(P/S)	Hormone Therapy	(H)
Radiation	(R)	Remission/Prevention	(R/P)
Chemotherapy	(C)		

Some recipes can be used from pretreatment through remission. All recipes are pertinent for cancer prevention. The recipes are based on increased needs during each particular treatment and include nutrients that target the reduction of the side effects associated with that treatment. These side effects are identified with each recipe. It is important to remember that eating one meal, one time, will not resolve a side effect. This book is designed to be used daily for the best effects.

For example, during chemotherapy, taste changes occur that can result in decreased appetite, so we include seasonings like lemon and extra naturally occurring sweet flavor to enhance the taste. During radiation, skin repair and integrity is an issue, so we include foods that have a higher omega-3 fatty acid content. (Omega-3 has been shown to be absorbed better through foods than through supplements.) During hormone therapy, the withdrawal of hormones often leads to joint aches, pains, and hot flashes—mineral-dense foods are very helpful in this case. Finally, for remission and in prevention, we include a diet that is balanced but also includes high antioxidant concentrations to "mop" up damage that occurred during chemotherapy or, when aiming to reduce the risk of developing cancer, to reduce inflammation and other forms of oxidative stress.

We suggest that as you reach the end of one treatment you slowly transition to the next set of recipes, because side effects may take time to resolve. For example, going from eating steamed vegetables to eating raw vegetables while your digestive tract is still recovering may make digestive disturbances worse.

Most importantly, our recipes are meant to stimulate your appetite and please your senses, even through cancer treatment. Rest assured that we have put flavor front and center. The recipes are both delicious and full of healing abilities. What more can you ask for from foods at this time?

Here we go!

Once I finished treatment, I felt physically depleted and mentally shaken, but also overcome by a desire to be stronger. I read books on nutrition, and began to realize that food can be transformative for health. Now I make a weekly family meal plan, carve out sufficient time for food preparation and shopping, and eat mindfully. My energy is way up, my whole family is eating healthier, and my relationship with food has changed in a fundamental way. It sounds simple, but it wasn't. It was a revelation to me that my relationship to food could be so positive, that food could be a tool to help me realize my most important goals.

—*Sarah Dion*

SHOPPING LIST

- While we highly recommend organic where possible, we know it is hard to buy everything organic. However, do try to buy extra virgin olive oil, which means it is the first pressing of the olives.
- Most of the items we recommend are available at your local grocery or health food store. All of them are available through online retailers such as Amazon.com.
- Bob's Red Mill sells all the grains we mention. Local supermarkets may carry these products or may be willing to order them for you. Visit their website at www.bobsredmill.com to order directly or locate stores that carry their products.
- ENER-G Foods (www.ener-g.com) is one of the original gluten-free and hypoallergenic food manufacturers. Kroger and Whole Foods carry this brand. Use their website to locate more stores that carry their products or buy from them directly.
- Some items, such as grains, may be available in the bulk bin section of your grocery or health food store, enabling you to buy small amounts of items you may use less of, at a lower price.

Agave syrup

Arrowroot, a healthier alternative to corn starch

Beans, canned (such as chickpeas and white beans)

Berries, frozen and fresh

Bragg Liquid Aminos (This liquid protein concentrate contains all the essential amino acids, and in a compromised health state, it is a good way to ensure you are getting them.)

Cinnamon, ground and sticks

Coconut milk (regular, not light)

Coconut oil

Cumin, ground

Daiya shredded cheese (nondairy and non-soy; It melts and is tasty!)

Dill weed, dried

Earth Balance nondairy, non-soy margarine (no trans fat, no hydrogenated fat)

Extra virgin olive oil (EVOO)

Gluten-free pasta (such as quinoa or corn, Tinkiyada rice pasta, Thai rice noodles, or Soba 100% buckwheat noodles)

Grade B maple syrup

Lemons, lemon juice

Nut and seed butters (such as almond, peanut, cashew, or pumpkin)

Nuts, chopped or sliced (such as almonds or walnuts)

Red wine vinegar

Rice vinegar

Salt (such as iodized, kosher, and sea salt)

Seeds (such as pumpkin and sesame)

Sesame oil

Sriracha

Tamari soy sauce (no wheat)

Walnut oil (for higher temperature cooking)

Storage tip: To keep olive oil fresh and prevent it from turning rancid, keep it in the refrigerator in a wide mouth jar. Use a measuring spoon to take out the amount you need. It will solidify in the refrigerator and melt very quickly.

Useful Equipment

Blender (for smoothies)

Coffee grinder (for grinding nuts)

Glad ® ClingWrap (does not contain harmful plasticizers that can leak into food and mimic estrogen. Never microwave in plastic containers for the same reason.)

Glass containers (for storage)

Immersion blender

Juicer

Muffin pans and liners

Parchment paper (makes clean up so much easier)

Slow cooker, such as a Crock-Pot

The very least you can do in your life is figure out what you hope for. And the most you can do is live inside that hope. Not admire it from a distance but live right in it, under its roof.

—Barbara Kingsolver

BREAKFAST

Creamy Rice Pudding

Grits and Eggs

Cheese Omelet with Veggies and Greens

Stewed Fruit

Oat Scones

Pear and Almond Muesli

Quinoa and Cinnamon Cereal

Savory Oatmeal

Steak and Eggs

Breakfast Vegetable Medley

French Toast with Nut Butter

Amaranth with Spices

One of the best things you can do for yourself during cancer treatment and for prevention is to eat a nutritious breakfast within a couple of hours of waking. Here's why: While we sleep our bodies depend on energy stores, primarily in the liver, to keep blood glucose levels balanced. By the time we wake, the liver is nearly depleted and depends on external sources of food to maintain proper blood sugar.

In addition to maintaining proper blood sugar levels, eating a nutritious breakfast can jump-start your immune system, assist in hydration, and help maintain good moods and stable weight. The brain is also highly dependent on glucose for cognitive functioning.

During radiation and chemotherapy, the repair and restoration of cells and tissue increase our need for protein. These therapies cause increased turnover and elimination of protein that will need to be replaced through the diet.

Chemotherapy, and the steroids given in conjunction, often lead to disruptions in metabolism that affect glucose balance and certainly affect thought processes and memory. To combat these disruptions we need to eat a breakfast with adequate amounts of long-term energy fuels, namely protein and fats, at the center.

Chemotherapy depresses the immune system. This vital system needs to actively survey the body for tumor cells, even during treatment. For the immune system to work properly we need to provide these cells with nutrients and amino acids from protein.

Taking pills to decrease pain after surgery or relieve acid reflux can lead to digestive problems such as nausea and constipation. A good breakfast can help to kick-start bowel regularities and optimize nutrient absorption.

Hot flashes and muscle aches are the most common associated side effects of hormone therapy. Controlling blood sugar and optimizing protein intake first thing in the morning can be extremely helpful in alleviating these side effects.

During conventional therapy we want weight to remain stable. But with the disruptions in fat metabolism associated with steroid use, there is a tendency to gain weight. And sometimes, particularly with gastrointestinal cancer surgeries and treatments, the concern is weight loss. Eating complementary breakfasts containing macronutrients is key in stabilizing weight.

By eating a balanced breakfast, fatigue can be better managed, and when the body does not have to rely on muscle for its protein, you won't lose the muscle mass that helps to maintain stamina.

We invite you to enjoy these delicious and highly nutritious recipes.

I have become so much more aware of the food I eat. Before diagnosis I didn't worry too much about processed foods and artificial sweeteners and junk food. Once chemo was over I started eating a healthier diet, paying more attention to the ingredients in my food. When one day I stopped at a local burger place because I was in a hurry, not only did it not taste as good as I remembered, my stomach was upset all night. Now I try to eat as organic as I can. (OK, I confess, I still have the occasional sugar binge; and yes, I feel terrible after!)

—Cherie Enholm

Creamy Rice Pudding

The rich, creamy texture of rice pudding makes it a popular comfort food. Replacing white rice with basmati brown rice, a whole grain, delivers fiber and a healthy dose of complex carbohydrates. Add dried cranberries for a boost of antioxidants.

....

Targeted Side Effects: Diarrhea, fatigue, insomnia, nausea

Calories: 170; Total Fat: 1 g; Saturated Fat: 0 g; Total Carbohydrate: 37 g; Total Fiber: 2 g; Protein: 2 g

....

Makes 4 servings
Ingredients:

¾ cup uncooked basmati brown rice, rinsed

1¼ cups water

2 cups regular coconut milk, divided

⅓ cup agave syrup or Grade B maple syrup

¼ teaspoon iodized salt

1 egg (shell rinsed), beaten

1 tablespoon nondairy, non-soy margarine (we prefer Earth Balance)

½ teaspoon vanilla extract

Optional: ⅔ cup golden raisins, regular raisins, or dried cranberries

Directions:

1. Bring rice and water to a boil in a medium saucepan. Reduce heat to low, cover, and simmer for 12 minutes.

2. Combine partially cooked rice, 1¼ cups coconut milk, agave, and salt. Cook over medium heat, stirring frequently until thick and creamy, 15 to 20 minutes.

3. Stir in remaining ¾ cup coconut milk, beaten egg, and raisins or cranberries, if using. Cook 10 minutes more, stirring constantly.

4. Remove from heat, spoon into bowl, and stir in margarine and vanilla. Serve hot or cold.

Health Tip 101: *Basmati brown rice is high in magnesium and selenium, both helpful in decreasing achiness in joints and muscles.*

Grits and Eggs

Eggs are a good source of protein and corn grits, as well as the very similar polenta, are the perfect complement for a balanced breakfast. And they do an excellent job soaking up the egg yolk!

....

Targeted Side Effects: Fatigue, blood sugar regulation, peripheral neuropathy

A good source of iron

Calories: 200; Total Fat: 7 g; Saturated Fat: 2 g; Total Carbohydrates: 23 g; Fiber: 1 g; Protein: 8 g

....

Makes 4 servings
Ingredients:

½ teaspoon iodized salt

3 cups water

1 cup whole kernel corn grits

1½ tablespoons nondairy, non-soy margarine (we prefer Earth Balance), divided

4 eggs (shells rinsed)

Health Tip 101: *Corn grits are high in vitamins C and A, and the antioxidant carotenoids lutein—associated with decreasing the risk of prostate cancer—and zeaxanthin.*

Directions:

1. Bring 3 cups of water and salt to a boil.

2. Add 1 cup corn grits and reduce heat. Cook slowly for 20 minutes, or until grits are tender and cooked through, stirring often. (The coarser the grits, the longer they will need to cook.)

3. Remove from heat, cover and let stand for a couple of minutes before serving.

4. While the grits rest, heat 2 teaspoons margarine in a frying pan over medium heat until melted. Break eggs and slip into pan, one at a time. Reduce heat to low. Cook slowly until whites are completely set and yolks begin to thicken but are not hard, about five to six minutes.

5. To serve, divide grits among four plates, stir in ½ teaspoon margarine to each serving, and top with an egg.

Cheese Omelet with Veggies and Greens

Loaded with veggies, leafy greens, and "cheese," this omelet is a protein- and nutrient-packed way to start your day.

....

Targeted Side Effects: Fatigue, blood sugar regulation, peripheral neuropathy, chemo brain

A good source of vitamin A, calcium, and iron

Calories: 430; Total Fat: 26 g; Saturated Fat: 6 g; Total Carbohydrates: 29 g; Fiber: 5 g; Protein: 40 g

....

Makes 2 servings
Ingredients:

1 tablespoon nondairy, non-soy margarine (we prefer Earth Balance) or olive oil, divided

½ onion, chopped

⅓ pepper, chopped or sliced

A big handful of spinach, chard, or dinosaur kale, chopped (if using frozen spinach, defrost and squeeze out excess water)

4 eggs (shells rinsed)

¼ cup nondairy milk

Small tomato, sliced

¼ cup shredded nondairy, non-soy mozzarella cheese (we prefer Daiya)

Salt and pepper, to taste

Health Tip 101: *Tomatoes are high in several important antioxidants, such as lutein. Lutein boosts eye health by protecting damage done by free radicals. Tomatoes also contain good amounts of chromium, which helps to keep blood sugar levels under control.*

Directions:

1. Heat frying pan over medium-low heat. Add ½ tablespoon margarine or olive oil. Raise heat to medium. Add chopped onion and pepper. Sauté, and stir until softened.

2. Add chopped leafy greens. Cover.

3. Crack eggs into a bowl. Season with salt and pepper to taste. Add milk and beat with a whisk or fork. Mix in cheese.

4. Remove cover from frying pan and add remaining margarine or olive oil to prevent eggs from sticking to pan. Pour in egg mixture. Cook for one minute. Top with tomato and sprinkle with cheese. Put lid back on pan, and turn heat to medium-low.

5. Check in 90 seconds, rolling loose eggs on top of pan toward sides to cook faster. Turn to low heat and keep watch until eggs are cooked.

6. Flip one side of the omelet over the other side in pan and serve.

Season with iodized salt and pepper to taste.

Stewed Fruit

This is an old family recipe to relieve constipation. It's also a good way to use fruit that may be getting too soft. A bowl of stewed fruit is a good way to start your day but is also a tasty snack. Store in the refrigerator for up to a week.

Targeted Side Effects: Constipation, fatigue, wound healing, anemia

High in vitamins A and C

Calories: 170; Total Fat: 0 g ; Saturated Fat: 0 g ; Total Carbohydrate: 41 g; Fiber: 4 g; Protein: 2 g

Equipment:

Optional: slow cooker

Makes 8 servings

Ingredients:

2 pounds of a combination of prunes, raisins, dried or fresh apricots, blueberries, apples, pears, plums, nectarines, or peaches, cut into chunks

¼ to ½ cup water

Optional: ½ teaspoon cinnamon

Directions:

1. Heat fruit and water in a covered pot over medium-low heat until some of the fruit renders its liquid. The bottom of the pot should have a couple of inches of liquid in it.

2. Raise heat to medium and stir once or twice. Add cinnamon if desired.

3. When mixture starts to bubble, turn heat down to simmer and cook, covered, until fruit is soft, about 20 to 30 minutes.

4. Remove from heat, uncover, and let cool. Serve warm, room temperature, or chilled.

To make in a slow cooker: Add all of the fruit and ⅓ cup water to slow cooker and leave it to cook on low for 6 hours—though you can't overcook it!

Health Tip 101: *Apricots and plums contain high levels of elemental iron, which can aid in preventing anemia. Elemental iron from food usually does not cause constipation.*

Oat Scones

These light, crumbly scones are always a hit. They are best served warm with jam. A light spread of margarine works well, too. When scones have cooled completely, wrap tightly with Glad wrap or place in an airtight container and store in the refrigerator for up to three days.

....

Targeted Side Effect: Fatigue

A good source of calcium

Calories: 140; Total Fat: 1.5 g; Saturated Fat: 0 g; Total Carbohydrates:–30 g; Fiber: 3 g; Protein: 4 g

....

Makes 8 servings
Ingredients:

1¾ cup Bob's Red Mill Gluten-Free Biscuit and Baking Mix, or any combination of brown rice flour, bean flour, or sorghum flour

½ cup rolled oats

2 teaspoons baking powder

½ teaspoon baking soda

¼ teaspoon iodized salt

2 tablespoons nondairy, non-soy margarine (we prefer Earth Balance)

2 tablespoons applesauce

1 egg (shell rinsed)

¾ cup plain nondairy milk, soured with juice of ½ lemon to make buttermilk

1 tablespoon agave syrup or Grade B maple syrup

¼ cup dried fruit such as raisins, cranberries, or cherries

Jam, for serving

Directions:

Preheat oven to 350°F

1. Grease a cookie sheet or an 8- to 9-inch pie pan with margarine or oil.

2. Combine dry ingredients in a big bowl.

3. Cut in margarine and applesauce.

4. Beat milk and egg. Add agave and stir until mixed. Add wet ingredients to dry ingredients, being careful not to over stir. Combine just until all ingredients are moist.

5. Pour batter onto cookie sheet or pie pan. Shape into a circle. Lightly score into eight pieces with a sharp knife. Do not cut all the way through.

6. Bake for 15 minutes, or until a toothpick comes out dry from the center. Serve warm with jam.

Health Tip 101: *Oats are high in both soluble and insoluble fiber, useful in maintaining proper bowel function and keeping your cholesterol in balance. Oats also contain about 9 grams of protein per cup.*

Pear and Almond Muesli

This simple meal is filling and tasty. The pears add a pleasing touch of sweetness to this savory dish.

Targeted Side Effects: Constipation, insomnia, fatigue, blood sugar regulation

Calories: 220; Total Fat: 5 g; Saturated Fat: 0 g; Total Carbohydrates: 41 g; Fiber: 7 g; Protein: 5 g

Makes 1 serving
Ingredients:

½ cup rolled oats

½ cup almond milk

1 pear, cored and chopped

2 tablespoons sliced almonds

¼ teaspoon cinnamon

2 teaspoons agave syrup

Directions:

1. Soak oats in almond milk for eight minutes.

2. Add chopped pear, sliced almonds, cinnamon, and agave. Mix all ingredients together and enjoy.

Health Tip 101: *Almonds provide a very good source of omega-3 fatty acids and vitamin E. Both nutrients are helpful in skin repair.*

Quinoa and Cinnamon Cereal

This delicious and hearty morning meal has a satisfying nutty flavor. Cinnamon adds warmth and depth.

Targeted Side Effects: Fatigue, blood sugar regulation, insomnia, nausea

High in iron and vitamin A and a good source of calcium

Calories: 140; Total Fat: 1.5 g; Saturated Fat: 0 g; Total Carbohydrate: 30 g; Fiber: 3 g; Protein: 4 g

Makes 1 serving
Ingredients:

2 cups water

½ cup quinoa

½ cup oatmeal

6 to 8 walnuts, chopped

1 tablespoon dried cranberries

1 tablespoon fresh or dried blueberries

1 tablespoon agave syrup or Grade B maple syrup

Cinnamon, to taste

Directions:

1. In a large pot, bring water to a boil.

2. Add quinoa and oatmeal, reduce heat, and simmer until water is absorbed, about 20 minutes.

3. Remove from heat. Stir in remaining ingredients and serve immediately.

Health Tip 101: *Quinoa contains a complete complement of protein (all the amino acids), fiber, and iron. All these nutrients are important for maintaining muscle mass and restoring red blood cells.*

Savory Oatmeal

Oatmeal is usually served as a sweet dish with fruit and maple syrup but you won't be disappointed in this savory version with mushrooms, eggs, and gomasio. High in protein and fiber, gomasio is a dry condiment made from organic sesame seeds and seaweed. Often used in Japanese cuisine, it can be found in the Asian food section of your grocery store or online.

Targeted Side Effects: Wound healing, skin and hair damage, constipation, insomnia

A good source of iron

Calories: 310; Total Fat: 12 g; Saturated Fat: 2 g; Total Carbohydrates: 30 g; Fiber: 4 g; Protein: 14 g

Makes 2 servings
Ingredients:

2 cups water

1 cup rolled or steel cut oats

⅓ cup sliced mushrooms, preferably cremini

¼ teaspoon ground cumin

1 tablespoon gomasio (or substitute 1 tablespoon sesame seeds and ¼ teaspoon sea salt or 1 teaspoon crumbled seaweed like dulse or nori)

½ tablespoon nondairy, non-soy margarine (we prefer Earth Balance)

1 tablespoon Bragg's Liquid Amino Acids or tamari

2 eggs (shells rinsed)

1 tablespoon shredded nondairy, non-soy cheese (we prefer Daiya)

Directions:

1. In a large pot, bring water to a boil and add oats. Turn down to medium-low heat. Stir.

2. Mix in sliced mushrooms, Bragg's or tamari, cumin, and gomasio. Turn down to simmer, stirring frequently. Cook until oats reach your desired texture and consistency, 15 to 20 minutes. Remove from heat and cover to keep warm.

3. Heat margarine in a frying pan over medium heat until melted. Break eggs and slip into pan, one at a time. Reduce heat to low. Cook slowly until whites are completely set and yolks begin to thicken but are not hard, about five to six minutes.

4. Distribute the oatmeal between two bowls and place a fried egg on top. Sprinkle with cheese shreds and serve immediately.

Health Tip 101: *Cumin is a very good source of iron and vitamin C. Vitamin C is an antioxidant that aids in decreasing stress and works to boost the immune system. It has been shown to stimulate digestive enzymes and aid nutrient absorption. Cumin also helps regulate blood sugar, reducing the chances of hypoglycemia.*

Steak and Eggs

You can—and should—have steak and eggs for breakfast. The protein in this recipe will keep you going all morning.

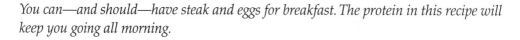

Targeted Side Effects: Fatigue, anemia, chemo brain, wound healing, peripheral neuropathy

A good source of iron

Calories: 360; Total Fat: 18 g; Saturated Fat: 6 g; Total Carbohydrate: 3 g; Fiber: 0 g; Protein: 40 g

Makes 1 serving
Ingredients:

⅛ teaspoon sea salt

3 ounces thin, boneless, hormone-free beef steak such as chuck or round (no minute steak)*

1 to 2 eggs (shells rinsed)

Pepper, to taste

Turmeric, to taste

Optional: condiments such as salsa, ketchup, and hot sauce

Directions:

1. Add salt to frying pan over medium heat.

2. When pan is hot, add steak and season with pepper and turmeric. You can add 2 tablespoons of water here to prevent sticking if necessary. In two minutes, turn steak over and cook for one more minute.

3. Break eggs into pan on top of steak. Cover. Cook steak and eggs to desired doneness. Serve with preferred condiments.

*Minute steaks and other meats that have been tenderized have been shown to have higher levels of bacteria. Tenderized meat should be avoided by anyone with a compromised immune system.

Health Tip 101: *Eggs contain protein and folate, essential for regenerating damaged tissues and immune cells.*

Breakfast Vegetable Medley

This wonderful breakfast side dish, a medley of mineral-rich vegetables and spices known to have dynamic healing properties, was created by Dr. Price's father, Jim Price. He eats this every morning and usually makes a large batch at the beginning of the week to reheat each day. This dish stores well in the refrigerator for up to a week.

Targeted Side Effects: Fatigue, blood sugar regulation, wound healing, hot flashes/night sweats

High in vitamins A and C and a good source of iron

Calories: 170; Total Fat: 8 g; Saturated Fat: 1.5 g; Total Carbohydrates: 21 g; Fiber: 18 g; Protein: 4 g

Makes 6 to 8 servings
Ingredients:

½ cup chopped red bell peppers

2 cups chopped bok choy

½ cup chopped leeks

½ cup chopped celery

½ cup chopped green apple

1 cup chopped yellow squash

1 cup chopped zucchini

2 cloves garlic, minced

1 tablespoon fresh ginger, minced

2 tablespoons chopped fennel bulb

1 tablespoon turmeric

½ teaspoon cumin, powdered

1 tablespoon olive oil or enough to coat the pan

¼ cup water

Directions:

1. In a bowl, combine all chopped vegetables, apple, and spices; toss until coated.

2. Heat olive oil in frying pan over medium heat. Sauté vegetable and apple mixture until slightly softened, about 5 to 10 minutes.

3. Pour water into mixture, cover, and cook for another five minutes to steam and soften the mixture.

4. Turn off the heat and let sit another five minutes to continue the softening process. Serve warm, at room temperature, or chilled.

Health Tip 101: *Leeks contain ample amounts of antioxidants that are converted to a compound called allicin. Allicin has been found to have antibacterial and antifungal properties. Leeks are also a great source of minerals and vitamins such as folate, niacin, and riboflavin.*

French Toast with Nut Butter

If you don't like to "eat" eggs, try this recipe. You'll get the protein and good fats from them without the taste or texture. The nut butter adds flavor but doesn't raise glucose levels and helps to lower the glycemic index of the meal.

Targeted Side Effects: Fatigue, chemo brain, wound healing

A good source of iron

Calories: 270; Total Fat: 16 g; Saturated Fat: 2 g; Total Carbohydrates: 26 g; Fiber: 2 g; Total Protein: 6 g

Makes 2 servings
Ingredients:

1 egg (shell rinsed)

⅓ cup nondairy milk

2 slices gluten-free bread (we recommend any of Udi's gluten-free sliced breads or Ener-G food's raisin bread)

¾ tablespoon nondairy, non-soy margarine (we prefer Earth Balance)

1½ tablespoons any nut butter

Optional: ½ teaspoon vanilla (if you don't use flavored milk)

Optional: Mixed berries

Directions:

1. Beat egg and milk together in a medium bowl. Add vanilla if desired.

2. Soak each slice of bread in egg mixture until well saturated.

3. In a large skillet over low-medium heat, melt margarine. Add soaked bread to skillet and cook until browned. Be careful not to burn. Flip over and repeat.

4. Serve with nut butter spread on top of each slice.

   Sprinkle with mixed berries, if desired.

Health Tip 101: *Tahini, the crushed butter of sesame seeds, can be used as one of the nut butters here. It is one of the best sources of elemental calcium and is high in protein. Recent studies have shown the benefits of sesame seeds as an anti-inflammatory.*

Amaranth with Spices

This recipe is from Jennifer Adler, MS, CN. Susan first tasted it at Jennifer's class for people with cancer and their families (www.passionatenutrition.com). Amaranth, an ancient grain from South America like quinoa and teff, is easy to digest. If you've never cooked with amaranth before, this flavorful recipe is an easy way to add a new grain to your food "tool box." Serve with Balsamic Blueberries (page 104).

Targeted Side Effects: Fatigue, wound healing, blood sugar regulation, hot flashes/night sweats

High in iron

Calories: 180; Total Fat: 3 g; Total Saturated Fat: 1 g; Total Carbohydrates: 31 g; Fiber: 13 g; Protein: 7 g

Makes 4 servings
Ingredients:

1 cup amaranth

⅛ teaspoon sea salt

1 cup of water

½ teaspoon cinnamon

½ teaspoon ground ginger

Directions:

1. Toast the amaranth in a saucepan over medium-low heat, stirring constantly, for four minutes, or until it starts to pop and emits a toasty aroma. Add sea salt.

2. Bring the water to a boil over high heat. Add the toasted amaranth, cinnamon, and ginger.

3. Cover, lower the heat and simmer for seven minutes, or until all the liquid has been absorbed.

4. Remove from heat and leave covered for 5 to 10 minutes before serving. Serve warm.

Health Tip 101: *Amaranth is a grain that is high in protein. It is also high in the amino acid lysine which helps convert fatty acids into energy and can counteract the effects of steroids on fat retention.*

Hope begins in the dark, the stubborn hope that if you just show up and try to do the right thing, the dawn will come.

—*Anne Lamott*

LUNCH

Borscht

Bangers and Mash

Dandelion and Arugula Salad

Split Pea Soup

Chickpea and Coconut Soup

Mushroom Buckwheat Soup

Cold Eggplant Salad

Quinoa Salad

Kale Salad

Rice Pasta with Sugar Snap Peas, Peanuts, and Asparagus

Pasta with Pesto

Frittata with Spinach, Mushrooms, and Onions

Mac and Cheese with Sausage

Mushroom Soup with Onions

Carrot Soup with Fennel

Salad Niçoise

Fall Bounty Squash Soup

Eloise's Salmon Patties

Sesame Noodles with Broccoli and Carrots

Bibimbap

Stuffed Portobello Mushrooms

Artichoke, Bean, Hazelnut, and Asparagus Salad

....

Midday is the time to stop, check in, refuel, and reflect on your stress and energy levels. It is also time to make sure that you are well hydrated.

By this time of the day, most people have entered into their daily routine, which often includes increased physical and brain activity. Inevitably, you've experienced some degree of stress. These activities consume quite a bit of nutrients and demand and deplete glucose. In fact, over the course of the morning, you've probably used much of the energy supplied by breakfast. Some of it may have been used to refuel the liver for the evening fast. It's now time to replenish nutrient stores to carry on through the day and avoid afternoon fatigue and slumps.

Not eating lunch can lead to internal stress, including increased epinephrine and cortisol secretion, as blood sugar levels decrease. Missing lunch may increase acid reflux, peripheral neuropathy, and symptoms of anxiety and depression, as well as depression of the immune system. Staying fed at lunch time helps to promote sleep, maintain good mood, and keep your metabolism active. Skipping lunch and waiting for the evening meal can lead to insulin spikes, which are not helpful to fighting cancer. Eating a healthful lunch will also help to close any nutrient deficiencies you may be experiencing. Team these main entrées with one of our side dishes for a more robust meal.

Being faced with the realization of my own mortality, and the fear that this could potentially be in a future not so distant, laden with treatment and pain, resulted in a need to live each day with burning passion: to love harder and speak louder; to have my voice heard; to stand up and clap the loudest, and to sit down and pray the hardest; to rejoice in the moments like I never have before. For the first time in my life, I found out how to truly live.

—Renae Wilbur

Borscht

Susan's grandfather managed a beet ranch in Russia before immigrating to the United States, so it's in her genes to love beets, hot or cold. This soup can be served both ways. Like most soups, this one tastes even better if you let it simmer longer and give the flavors time to combine before serving. Borscht keeps for several days in the refrigerator and freezes well for up to two weeks.

....

Targeted Side Effects: Constipation, fatigue, anemia

A good source of vitamins A and C

Calories: 160; Total Fat: 8 g; Saturated Fat: 3 g; Total Carbohydrates: 21 g; Fiber: 3 g; Protein: 4 g

....

Makes 8 servings
Ingredients:

4 cups vegetable or beef broth

1 (14.5-ounce) can stewed tomatoes with juice

1½ cups thinly sliced or shredded napa or savoy cabbage

¾ cup thinly sliced carrots

¾ cup sliced onions

2 teaspoons kosher salt

⅛ teaspoon pepper

1 teaspoon agave syrup

2 large russet potatoes with skin on, cut into quarters

8 ounces lean beef (such as stewing beef)

1½ cups peeled raw beets cut into matchsticks

2 teaspoons lemon juice

2 teaspoons dried dill weed, more to taste

Optional: Nondairy sour cream

Directions:

1. In a large soup pot, bring broth, stewed tomatoes, cabbage, carrots, onions, salt, and pepper to a boil. Reduce heat to low, cover, and simmer for 15 minutes.

2. Stir in agave, potatoes, beef, beets, and dill. Cover and cook over medium heat for 20 minutes. Add lemon juice.

3. When potatoes are cooked, (a fork goes in easily) remove from pot and set aside.

4. Serve warm or cold in soup bowls with a potato chunk on top and a dollop of sour cream, if desired.

Health Tip 101: *One serving of cabbage contains 61% RDA of vitamin C. It also contains vitamins B5, B6, B1, and K as well as the phytonutrient indole-3-carbinol, shown to help reduce hot flashes.*

Bangers and Mash

A healthier version of the traditional British dish of sausages and mashed potatoes. During World War I soldiers cooked sausages over an open fire and they popped as they cooked. Hence, the name "bangers." Here, mashed cauliflower adds nutrients and provides the texture of potatoes without raising your blood sugar. Serve with Kale Salad (page 26).

Targeted Side Effects: Fatigue, wound healing, hot flashes/night sweats

A good source of vitamin C and iron

Calories: 280; Total Fat: 17 g; Saturated Fat: 4.5 g; Total Carbohydrates: 16 g; Fiber: 6 g; Protein: 18 g

Equipment:
Blender, immersion blender, or food processor

Makes 4 servings

Ingredients:

3 cups water

1 to 2 heads of cauliflower, trimmed and cut into florets (stems can be reserved for soups or discarded)

½ teaspoon sea salt

3 cloves garlic, chopped

4 non-nitrate, non-nitrite, hormone-free sausages

½ tablespoon olive oil

2 tablespoons nondairy, non-soy margarine (we prefer Earth Balance)

Directions:

1. Boil water in a large pot. Add the cauliflower, sea salt, and garlic and cover. After returning to a boil, turn down heat to medium. Cook until florets are soft, 8 to 10 minutes. Drain cauliflower in a colander and set aside. Reserve 2 to 3 tablespoons of the cooking water.

2. Meanwhile, heat olive oil in a skillet over medium heat. Add sausages and cook, covered, turning every three minutes to brown them on all sides.

3. As the sausages are browning, place cauliflower into a blender or food processor (if using an immersion blender, transfer to a bowl). Add margarine, salt, and 1 tablespoon cooking water. Blend until smooth or your preferred consistency is reached. Add more cooking water if necessary.

Health Tip 101: *Cauliflower is a good source of several B vitamins and omega-3 fatty acids. These nutrients help decrease anxiety and increase calmness and good moods.*

Dandelion and Arugula Salad

This refreshing nutrient dense salad is filled with vegetables found in late spring and throughout the summer. It has a nutty flavor with a slight burst of sweetness from the fresh raspberries.

Targeted Side Effects: Constipation, loss of appetite, anemia

A good source of calcium and high in iron, vitamin A, and vitamin C

Calories: 430; Total Fat: 39 g; Saturated Fat: 4.5 g; Total Carbohydrates: 20 g; Fiber: 8 g; Protein: 7 g

Makes 2 servings

Ingredients:

1 cup of arugula

1 cup dandelion greens

1 cup spinach

½ cup fresh raspberries

½ avocado, sliced

½ cup hazelnuts, ground or chopped

2 tablespoons olive oil

2 tablespoons balsamic vinegar

1 tablespoon lemon juice

Directions:

1. Combine the greens, raspberries, avocado, and hazelnuts in a bowl.

2. In a separate smaller bowl, mix together the oil, vinegar, and lemon juice.

3. Toss salad with dressing. Enjoy.

Health Tip 101: *Dandelion greens are considered bitters, which help to stimulate digestion and aid proper bowel function. In addition, dandelion leaves provide a good source of iron and electrolytes.*

Split Pea Soup

This hearty, velvety soup tastes even better if you let the soup simmer longer and give the flavors time to combine before serving. It's wonderful the next day, keeps in the fridge for up to five days, and freezes well. It's excellent paired with our Papaya Salad (page 72).

....

Targeted Side Effects: Fatigue, fat metabolism, hot flashes/night sweats

High in vitamin A

Calories: 120; Total Fat: 0 g; Saturated Fat: 0 g; Total Carbohydrates: 22 g; Fiber: 8 g; Protein: 7 g

....

Equipment:
Blender, immersion blender, or food processor.

Optional: slow cooker

Makes 6 servings

Ingredients:

1 cup dry split peas, rinsed

5 cups vegetable or chicken broth

2 large carrots, cut into rounds

2 stalks of celery with leaves, chopped

1 medium onion, sliced

1 teaspoon sea salt

½ teaspoon black or white pepper

Directions:

1. Place broth and dry split peas in a soup pot and bring to a low boil.

2. After reaching a boil, turn down heat to simmer and add the rest of ingredients. Cover and cook for one to two hours or until soup turns thick.

3. Remove soup from heat and allow to cool slightly. Using a hand-held immersion blender, blender, or food processor, process until smooth. Serve hot.

To make in a slow cooker: Place broth and dry split peas in a slow cooker, turn on high and cover. When soup boils, turn heat down to low and cook for two to three hours.

Health Tip 101: *Peas are high in soluble fiber and help to stabilize blood sugar levels.*

Chickpea and Coconut Soup

Coconut milk has many positive properties. Although it is a saturated fat, it doesn't go through the liver to be digested so it's easier to digest, making it especially useful for people with tender tummies. Chickpeas add needed fiber and protein. The soup stores in the refrigerator in a covered container for up to two days.

Targeted Side Effects: Fatigue, hot flashes

High in iron and a good source of vitamin A

Calories: 410; Total Fat: 26 g; Saturated Fat: 20 g; Total Carbohydrates: 37 g; Fiber: 10 g; Protein: 13 g

Equipment:
Blender or food processor

Makes 4 to 5 servings
Ingredients:

2 (14.5-ounce) cans of chickpeas

2 cups of chicken or vegetable broth

2 cloves garlic

15 ounces of regular coconut milk

1 teaspoon ground cumin

1 teaspoon agave syrup

2 cups Swiss chard, cut into strips

1 tablespoon curry powder

Salt and pepper, to taste

Optional: corn or gluten-free tortillas

Directions:

1. In a blender or food processor, puree chickpeas, garlic, coconut milk, curry powder, cumin, and agave until smooth.

2. Transfer mixture to a pot and place over low heat. Add Swiss chard. Simmer, stirring occasionally, until Swiss chard is tender and soup is heated through, about 10 minutes.

3. Remove from heat, season with salt and pepper to taste, and serve in bowls.

Health Tip 101: *Chickpeas contain healthy amounts of molybdenum, a nutrient helpful in detoxifying sulfites from the body. These protein-rich beans also contain folate and iron. High in fiber, chickpeas can help you maintain proper bowel movements and curb an appetite that may be stimulated by steroids.*

Mushroom Buckwheat Soup

Substituting buckwheat for barley makes this soup gluten free. Mushrooms strengthen the immune system and contain Vitamin D^3, which is good for bone and kidney support. This hearty soup can be stored in the refrigerator for up to four days and freezes well.

Targeted Side Effects: Wound healing, anemia, fatigue

A good source of iron

Calories: 160; Total Fat: 2 g; Saturated Fat: 0 g; Total Carbohydrate: 30 g; Fiber: 3 g; Protein: 7 g

Makes 8 servings

Ingredients:

1 cup buckwheat

4 cups vegetable broth, divided

2 potatoes, peeled and cubed

1 (14.5-ounce) can cannellini white beans

1 tablespoon olive oil, divided

Small onion, peeled, roughly chopped

1½ stalks of celery with leaves, roughly chopped

¾ pound sliced mushrooms, such as portobello, shiitake, cremini, or maitake

4 cups mushroom broth

1 teaspoon paprika

½ tablespoon coarse salt

Pepper, to taste

Directions:

1. Cook buckwheat and 1½ cups of vegetable broth in a large covered pot over medium heat for 20 minutes.

2. Add potatoes, beans, and remaining vegetable broth and continue cooking for 10 minutes.

3. Meanwhile, sauté onion and celery in ½ tablespoon of oil in a large frying pan over medium heat for five minutes. Add remaining oil and mushrooms and sauté for three minutes.

4. Add sautéed vegetables, mushroom broth, and paprika to soup pot with cooked buckwheat. Stir to blend. Season with salt and pepper to taste.

5. Cook for 15 minutes and serve hot.

Health Tip 101: *Buckwheat has a low glycemic index, essential for maintaining steady blood sugar. It is also high in both soluble and insoluble fiber, which promote optimal digestive health and contribute to decreasing the risk of some gastrointestinal cancers.*

Cold Eggplant Salad

Susan's husband's aunt made this salad and it was always a favorite. It's a great summer dish and keeps in the refrigerator for over a week. Pair it with our Lentil Loaf (page 49) for a complete meal with a Mediterranean twist.

Targeted Side Effects: Wound and skin healing, fatigue

A good source of vitamins A and C

Calories: 330; Total Fat: 30 g; Saturated Fat: 4.5 g; Total Carbohydrates: 15 g; Fiber: 7 g; Protein: 3 g

Makes 8 servings

Ingredients:

1 large eggplant

3 green onions or 1 small yellow or white onion, chopped

1 clove garlic, minced

½ cup olive oil

1½ tablespoons red wine vinegar or 1 tablespoon balsamic vinegar

¼ cup chopped fresh parsley

½ teaspoon iodized salt

Pepper, to taste

2 cups torn red lettuce leaves

8 to 16 tomato wedges or slices

16 pitted black or Kalamata olives

Optional: gluten-free crackers

Directions:

1. Bake eggplant at 350°F for 20 minutes or microwave until soft, about four minutes.

2. Remove skin and chop eggplant.

3. In a large bowl, combine eggplant, onion, garlic, olive oil, vinegar, parsley, salt, and pepper. Chill, covered in refrigerator. Serve cold.

4. To serve, scoop eggplant salad onto a bed of lettuce leaves. Garnish with tomatoes and black olives. Serve with crackers, if desired.

Health Tip 101: *Eggplant contains a number of antioxidants, including caffeic and chlorogenic acid, and the flavonoid nasunin, which promotes healthy brain function.*

Quinoa Salad

This recipe is a winner! Moist quinoa pairs well with the sharp tang of onion and red pepper and the brightness of lemon and fresh cilantro. This salad can be eaten by itself or paired with our Chickpea and Coconut Soup (page 22). Covered in the refrigerator, it stores well for three to four days. Most times, it gets eaten up before that!

....

Targeted Side Effects: Fatigue, blood sugar regulation, insomnia

A good source of vitamin C and iron

Calorie: 210; Total Fat: 11 g; Saturated Fat: 1.5 g; Total Carbohydrates: 23 g; Fiber: 3 g; Protein: 5 g

....

Makes 6 servings
Ingredients

1 cup quinoa

2 cups water

½ cup lemon juice

4 tablespoons olive oil

3 cloves garlic, minced

1 teaspoon sea salt

Pepper, to taste

½ cup cilantro without stems, finely chopped

4 green or 1 small red onions, chopped

1 red pepper, diced

½ cucumber, diced

Directions:

1. Bring quinoa and water to a boil and reduce heat. Simmer until water is absorbed, 10 to 15 minutes. Set aside to cool.

2. Whisk together lemon juice, oil, garlic, salt, and pepper.

3. Add onion, cilantro, red pepper, and cucumber to quinoa.

4. Pour lemon juice mixture over quinoa and vegetables, and toss. Serve at room temperature or chilled.

Health Tip 101: *Cilantro contains nutrients that are antibacterial and antihyperglycemic. This delicious spice assists the digestive system by stimulating the production of digestive enzymes. It also has antianxiety effects and can improve sleep quality.*

Kale Salad*

Kale and Brussels sprouts pair well with this lemon mustard dressing for a full-bodied salad that is high in nutrients and fiber. Pair this with our Frittata with Spinach, Mushrooms, and Onions (page 29) for a complete meal.

....

Targeted Side Effects: Hot flashes/night sweats, constipation, insomnia

A good source of vitamins A and C

Calories: 220; Total Fat: 15 g; Saturated Fat: 3 g; Total Carbohydrates: 17 g; Fiber: 23 g; Protein: 5 g

....

Makes 4 servings

Ingredients:

2 bunches of kale, stemmed and chopped into ½ inch pieces or smaller

1 bunch Brussels sprouts with the outer big leaves removed, chopped or shredded

1 cup slivered almonds

¾ cup shredded nondairy, non-soy cheese (we prefer Daiya)

Dressing:

2 lemons, juiced

1 teaspoon Dijon mustard

1 clove garlic, crushed and chopped

1 teaspoon oregano

¾ cup olive oil

Salt and pepper, to taste

Directions:

1. In a large bowl, combine kale, Brussels sprouts, almonds, and cheese. Set aside.

2. In another bowl, whisk the dressing ingredients together and season to taste.

3. Toss salad with dressing or serve on the side.

*This recipe is not recommended for patients on a low-fiber diet.

Health Tip 101: *Oregano contains the antioxidants thymol and rosamarinic acid that are antimicrobial and anti-inflammatory. On a gram weight basis oregano contains more antioxidants than blueberries. It is also a good source of iron and manganese, both helpful in the production of red blood cells.*

Rice Pasta with Sugar Snap Peas, Peanuts, and Asparagus

A quick and easy recipe that is sure to become a new comfort food favorite. It is healthy, balanced, and pleasing to the eye.

Targeted Side Effects: Fatigue, hot flashes, blood sugar regulation

High in vitamin C

Calories: 310; Total Fat: 15 g; Saturated Fat: 2.5 g; Total Carbohydrates: 40 g; Fiber: 4 g; Protein: 7 g

Makes 4 servings

Ingredients:

8 ounces uncooked small rice pasta such as rotini

1 tablespoon olive oil

¾ cup chopped white onion

2 cloves garlic, minced

16 asparagus spears, top half only (reserve bottom half for soup or stir fry)

1 lemon, juiced

5 ounces sugar snap peas (frozen are fine)

6 tablespoons shredded nondairy, non-soy cheese (we prefer Daiya)

¼ cup dry roasted, salted peanuts, roughly chopped

2 tablespoons nondairy, non-soy margarine, melted (we prefer Earth Balance)

1⅓ teaspoons salt or to taste

⅛ teaspoon white or black pepper

Directions:

1. Bring a large pot of salted water to a boil and cook pasta according to directions on package. Drain, reserving ½ cup pasta water.

2. In a large saucepan or wok, heat oil over medium heat. Add onion and stir until softened. Add garlic, snap peas, asparagus, and lemon juice. Cook, stirring frequently, for one minute.

3. Stir in cooked pasta and ½ cup pasta water, and cook until water is almost all absorbed and vegetables are bright green, about four minutes. Season with salt and pepper.

4. Divide pasta and vegetables into four bowls, top with shredded cheese and chopped peanuts. Drizzle with melted margarine and season with salt and pepper.

Health Tip 101: *Sugar peas are high in fiber. They also contain healthful amounts of vitamin K, a nutrient essential in osteopenia and osteoporosis prevention.*

Pasta with Pesto

You won't miss the dairy in this pesto sauce! Gluten-free pasta works better in shorter forms, so we recommend using rigatoni, macaroni, or shells in this recipe. Though if you are craving linguini, Thai rice noodles are an excellent substitution. For an added protein boost, serve with boiled shrimp or slices of baked chicken.

....

Targeted Side Effects: Fatigue, infection

Calories: 350; Total Fat: 32 g; Saturated Fat: 4 g; Total Carbohydrates: 16 g; Fiber: 3 g; Protein: 5 g

....

Equipment:
Blender, immersion blender, or food processor

Makes 4 servings

Ingredients:

1 cup fresh basil leaves

1 clove garlic, chopped

¾ cup raw walnuts or cashews

2 tablespoons nutritional yeast or ¼ cup shredded nondairy, non-soy mozzarella cheese (we recommend Daiya)

½ teaspoon salt, more if desired

Pepper, to taste

½ cup olive oil

8 ounces uncooked gluten-free pasta (such as quinoa or rice pasta)

Directions:

1. Using your equipment, pulse basil, garlic, nuts, nutritional yeast or cheese shreds, pepper, and salt until coarsely chopped, about 15 seconds. Drizzle in oil until all ingredients are thoroughly pureed and smooth. Use less oil for thicker pesto and more oil for thinner pesto.

2. Bring a pot of salted water to a boil. Add pasta and cook according to directions on package. Drain.

3. Plate pasta with pesto.

Health Tip 101: *Basil contains anti-inflammatory nutrients and antibacterial properties.*

Frittata with Spinach, Mushrooms, and Onions

This is a hearty meal, easy to make, and pretty on the plate. It's a well-balanced dish of good fat, carbohydrates, and protein.

Targeted Side Effects: Fatigue, wound healing, anemia

High in vitamin A, calcium, and iron and a good source of vitamin C

Calories: 320; Total Fat: 19 g; Saturated Fat: 4.5 g; Total Carbohydrates: 18 g; Fiber: 3 g; Total Protein: 16 g

Equipment:

oven-safe skillet

Makes 2 servings

Ingredients:

4 large eggs (shells rinsed)

¼ cup plain nondairy milk

¼ teaspoon sea salt

¼ teaspoon basil

¼ teaspoon oregano

¼ teaspoon dill weed

1 tablespoon olive oil, divided

½ onion, sliced and divided into rings

⅓ cup sliced mushrooms (shiitake or portobello preferred)

1 cup fresh or frozen spinach. If using frozen, defrost and squeeze out water

¼ cup shredded nondairy, non-soy mozzarella cheese (we prefer Daiya)

Pepper, to taste

Optional: 1 garlic clove, minced

Directions:

Preheat oven to 375°F

1. In a large bowl, whisk eggs, milk, salt, and pepper. Stir in herbs. Set aside.

2. Heat ½ tablespoon oil in skillet over medium heat. Add onions and mushrooms and cook until onions are translucent. Add garlic, if using, and cook for one minute.

3. Turn heat down to low. Drizzle remaining oil over bottom of pan. Pour egg mixture evenly over pan. Add spinach and shredded cheese (save some cheese for garnish, if desired). Cook covered for two to three minutes.

4. Remove cover and transfer to oven. Cook until eggs are completely set and cheese melts. Be careful not to overcook.

5. Remove frittata from oven, cut in half, sprinkle any remaining cheese on top of frittata, and serve.

Health Tip 101: *Spinach helps to stabilize blood sugar. It contains the nutrients choline and inositol, which help prevent thickening of the arteries.*

Mac and Cheese with Sausage

Your eyes are not deceiving you. With some slight alterations, this comfort food classic delivers the flavor you crave with added health benefits.

....

Targeted Side Effect: Fatigue

A good source of calcium

Calories: 470; Total Fat: 22 g; Saturated Fat: 6 g; Total Carbohydrates: 32 g; Fiber: 4 g; Protein: 12 g

....

Makes 6 servings

Ingredients:

8 ounces uncooked gluten-free pasta (such as rice or quinoa pasta)

¼ teaspoon iodized salt

2 tablespoons olive oil, divided

4 chicken and apple sausages, cut into thin slices

2 tablespoons gluten-free all-purpose flour or arrowroot

¼ teaspoon white pepper

2 cups almond or rice milk, preferably plain

2⅓ cups shredded nondairy, non-soy cheddar cheese

Health Tip 101: *Almond milk contains healthful amounts of magnesium, manganese, selenium, and vitamin E and is a wonderful dairy substitute for people who are lactose intolerant.*

Directions:

1. Bring a large pot of salted water to a boil and cook pasta according to directions on package until al dente or slightly undercooked. Drain. Rinse lightly under cool water. Set aside.

2. In a skillet with 2 teaspoons oil, cook sausage until both sides are browned.

3. In a large saucepan, heat remaining oil over low heat. Whisk in flour or arrowroot until well combined and starting to thicken, about two minutes. Season with pepper.

4. Raise heat to medium and add milk slowly, stirring constantly until there are no lumps. Blend in 2 cups shredded cheese, mixing until cheese is completely melted.

5. Stir in pasta and sausage slices. Serve immediately, sprinkling each serving with remaining cheese.

6. Optional: After adding the pasta and sausage to the cheese sauce, transfer to an oven-safe dish and bake at 350°F until lightly browned, 10 to 15 minutes. Start checking early to be sure the cheese doesn't burn.

Mushroom Soup with Onions

This soup has an earthy flavor and slightly creamy broth that is very satisfying. Keeps in the refrigerator for up to three days.

Targeted Side Effects: Fatigue, blood sugar regulation

High in vitamin C and calcium

Calories: 200; Total Fat: 9 g; Saturated Fat: 2.5 g; Total Carbohydrates: 27 g; Fiber: 6 g; Protein: 5 g

Makes 3 servings

Ingredients:

8 ounces fresh shiitake or portobello mushrooms, cleaned

2 tablespoons nondairy, non-soy margarine (we prefer Earth Balance)

1 onion, sliced into small discs

2 tablespoons gluten-free all-purpose flour or arrowroot

4 cups mushroom broth

Salt and pepper, to taste

Directions:

1. Coarsely chop mushrooms.

2. In medium saucepan over low heat, melt margarine. Add onions, stirring frequently until soft and light brown. Season with salt and pepper.

3. Add flour or arrowroot and gradually stir in broth, raising heat to medium. Keep stirring until soup thickens.

4. Ladle into bowls and serve hot.

Health Tip 101: *Onions contain chromium, which helps to regulate blood sugar. They also contain phytochemicals, including quercitin, which improve the function of vitamin C in the body.*

Carrot Soup with Fennel

We hope you fall in love with the rich orange color and rustic texture of this soup as much as we have. The ginger, fennel, and hint of orange mix to produce an alluring aroma, and it tastes even better. Keeps in the refrigerator for up to three days.

....

Targeted Side Effects: Constipation, wound healing, gas and bloating, nausea

High in vitamin A and a good source of vitamin C and iron

Calories: 250; Total Fat: 19 g; Saturated Fat: 7 g; Total Carbohydrates: 24 g; Fiber: 5 g Protein: 7 g

....

Equipment:
blender or food processor

Makes 4 to 6 servings

Ingredients:

1 medium fennel bulb, coarsely chopped

2 tablespoons coconut oil

1½ pounds carrots, sliced

1 clove garlic

1 teaspoon kosher salt

⅓ cup orange juice

2 tablespoons grated fresh ginger

¾ cup natural cashews

6 cups water, divided

Directions:

1. In blender or food processor, combine all ingredients and 3 cups of water and process until smooth.

2. Transfer to a large pot, add remaining water, and mix well.

3. Simmer over low heat for 30 minutes.

Health Tip 101: *Cashews, in addition to being a good source of protein, contain many helpful minerals for red blood cell production, including copper, magnesium, and iron.*

Salad Niçoise

A quick and easy summer dish that has all the components of a complete meal.

....

Targeted Side Effects: Fatigue, hot flashes, muscle aches

A good source of vitamin A

Calories: 200; Total Fat: 6 g; Saturated Fat: 1 g; Total Carbohydrates: 23 g; Fiber: 5 g; Protein: 13 g

....

Makes 2 to 4 servings

Ingredients:

½ head of romaine lettuce, washed and dried

1 to 2 cans light tuna* in water or oil, drained (if packed in oil, reserve oil for dressing)

20 black olives (Niçoise or Kalamata olives preferred)

3 Yukon gold potatoes, boiled and cut into chunks

½ pound green beans, washed, trimmed, and lightly steamed

2 to 3 tablespoons olive oil (including oil from tuna, if using)

2 lemons, juiced

⅛ teaspoon kosher salt

Pinch pepper

Directions:

1. Line small platter or large plate with lettuce leaves. Spread chunks of tuna over lettuce.

2. Arrange potatoes, black olives, and green beans around tuna on platter.

3. Whisk together olive oil, salt, pepper, and lemon juice for dressing.

4. Serve dressing on side or drizzle on top.

*Light tuna is lower in mercury than albacore.

Health Tips 101: *Olives are a good source of iron and are rich in fatty acids, an anti-inflammatory. They also contain vitamin E, which is important for skin health.*

Fall Bounty Squash Soup

This soup is a great example of "Eating from the Rainbow," combining many different fruits and vegetables into a yummy, versatile, and nutrient-packed soup. It keeps in the fridge for up to four days and freezes well for up to three weeks.

Targeted Side Effects: Constipation, wound healing

A good source of vitamins A and C

Calories: 160; Total Fat: 2 g; Saturated Fat: 0 g; Total Carbohydrates: 35 g; Fiber: 7 g; Protein: 2 g

Equipment:
Blender, immersion blender, or food processor

Makes 6 servings

Ingredients:

1 tablespoon olive oil

½ large white onion, cut into slices

4 cups vegetable broth, divided

2 cups butternut squash, skin removed (easier to work with if slightly softened in oven or microwave)

Any combination of these fruits and vegetables:

   2 carrots, cut in chunks

   2 large apples with skins, cut in chunks, seeds and core removed

   2 large pears with skins, cut in chunks, seeds and core removed

1 teaspoon ground cinnamon, more to taste

1½ teaspoons ground or 1 tablespoon minced fresh ginger

¼ teaspoon white or black pepper

½ teaspoon kosher salt

Optional: Nondairy sour cream

Directions:

1. In a large soup pot, heat olive oil over medium heat. Add onion slices and cook until onions turn translucent.

2. Add 1 cup of vegetable broth and your combination of fruits and vegetables. Cook until they start to soften.

3. Stir in spices, salt, and pepper.

4. Pour in rest of vegetable broth and simmer until all fruits and vegetables are soft. Remove soup from heat and allow to cool slightly. Using a hand-held immersion blender, blender, or food processor, process until smooth. Serve hot. Top with sour cream if desired.

Health Tip 101: *Squash is high in vitamins C and A, magnesium, folate, and copper. It also contains riboflavin, phosphorus, and vitamin K, as well as a healthful supply of electrolytes, which are essential for nerve and muscle function.*

Eloise's Salmon Patties

Dr. Price's maternal grandmother, Eloise, was a native of New Orleans who later moved to Brooklyn, New York, to raise her family. She insisted that meals be made from whole foods and not cans or packaged goods. Growing up, Dr. Price remembers eating these mouthwatering patties most Friday evenings. These patties go well with Sesame Noodles with Broccoli and Carrots (page 36).

Targeted Side Effects: Fatigue, joint pain, hot flashes/night sweats, insomnia, chemo brain

A good source of calcium

Calories: 360; Fat: 20 g; Saturated Fat: 4 g; Total Carbohydrates: 21 g; Fiber: 4 g; Protein: 22 g

Makes 5 servings

Ingredients:

1 pound of fresh or canned wild salmon

½ cup gluten-free bread crumbs

2 large eggs (shells rinsed)

½ large onion, grated

1 clove garlic, chopped fine

½ teaspoon of kosher salt, or more to taste

Fresh ground black pepper, to taste

3 tablespoons plain nondairy milk

3 tablespoons gluten-free all-purpose flour

1½ tablespoons olive oil

Directions:

1. To poach fresh salmon: Place fish in skillet with water about 1 inch high. Turn to medium heat. Cover. As water gets hot and steaming, the fish will cook from the steam in 8 to 10 minutes, depending on thickness (watch in case you have to add more water). Set aside.

2. In a large bowl, combine poached or canned salmon, bread crumbs, eggs, onion, garlic, salt, pepper, and milk. Mix thoroughly and form into five patties, each about 3 to 4 inches in diameter.

3. Dredge the patties through flour, coating both sides.

4. Heat olive oil in a large skillet over medium heat. Fry the patties for five minutes on each side, until brown.

5. Serve hot or at room temperature.

Health Tip 101: *Onions are a rich source of the antioxidant quercitin. Quercitin, found in many fruits and vegetables, prevents damage caused by inflammation and relieves hay fever.*

Sesame Noodles with Broccoli and Carrots

This recipe was adapted from Sesame Noodles with Broccoli by Maureen Callahan that appeared in the April 2007 issue of Cooking Light *magazine. Our version removes or replaces ingredients known to cause inflammation, such as soy sauce and honey, without sacrificing flavor.*

Targeted Side Effects: Hot flashes/night sweats, fatigue, joint aches, insomnia

A good source of iron

Calories: 290; Total Fat: 7 g; Saturated Fat: 1 g; Total Carbohydrates: 51 g; Fiber: 2 g; Protein: 4 g

Makes 4 servings

Ingredients:

8 ounces Thai rice noodles

1 medium broccoli, cut into small florets and peeled stem cut into rounds.

2 medium carrots, peeled and cut into matchsticks

Dressing:

2 tablespoons tahini (we prefer Joyva)

1 tablespoon sesame oil or olive oil

2 tablespoons rice vinegar

2 tablespoons water

1 tablespoon agave syrup

1 tablespoon tamari

Optional: Sriracha or hot sauce

1 tablespoon sesame seeds

Directions:

1. Bring a large pot of salted water to a boil. Add noodles and cook according to package directions. Drain.

2. Steam broccoli and carrots in a double boiler or steamer basket until tender, three to four minutes.

3. To make the dressing, in a small bowl, combine tahini, oil, vinegar, water, agave, and salt. Set aside.

4. In a large bowl, add broccoli, carrots, noodles, and sesame dressing. Toss to combine. To serve, divide into four plates or bowls. Drizzle with hot sauce and sprinkle with sesame seeds, if desired.

Health Tip 101: *Tahini, a paste made from sesame seeds, is very high in calcium and copper, essential nutrients for building bone and collagen.*

Balsamic Blueberries, p. 104

Roasted Brussels Sprouts with Garlic Sauce, p. 74

Borscht, p. 18

Coconut Fish Curry, p. 48

Bibimbap, p. 37

Artichoke, Bean, Hazelnut, and Asparagus Salad, p. 40

Quinoa Salad, p. 25

Salad Niçoise, p. 33

Grilled Tomatoes, p. 73

Oat Scones, p. 8

Mango Lassi, p. 112

Chili Paste Salmon, p. 44

Steak and Vegetable Fajitas, p. 46

Mushroom Buckwheat Soup, p. 23

Stuffed Portobello Mushrooms, p. 38

Sweet and Sour Baked Chicken, p. 59

Stuffed Peppers, p. 60

Roasted Vegetables, p. 71

Eloise's Salmon Patties, p. 35

Hummus with Turmeric, p. 91

Blueberry Smoothie, p. 93

Beet Spread with Sour Cream, Dill, and Horseradish, p. 90

Carrot, Ginger, and Arame Salad, p. 83

Zucchini and Carrot Muffins, p. 94

Banana with Chocolate and Walnuts, p. 100

Crispy Chewies, p. 103

Carob Fudge, p. 101

Pear and Almond Muesli, p. 9

Carrot Soup with Fennel, p. 32

Bibimbap

Bibimbap is a Korean rice dish traditionally topped with meat, vegetables, egg, and chili paste. Our version is inspired by Kim Kasner Stone's California-Style Bibimpap that appeared in the May 2013 issue of Sunset *magazine. Our lower inflammatory version uses brown jasmine rice, a whole grain, and less salt. It's become one of our favorite recipes because it is nutritionally complete, flavorful, beautiful on the plate, and simple to make.*

Targeted Side Effects: Fatigue, peripheral neuropathy, chemo brain

A good source of vitamins A and C, calcium, and iron

Calories: 440; Total Fat: 19 g; Saturated Fat: 3.31 g; Total Carbohydrate: 54 g; Fiber: 7 g; Protein: 15 g

Makes 4 servings
Ingredients:

1 cup jasmine brown rice, rinsed

2 tablespoons olive oil, divided

1 bunch kale or spinach, chopped

1 bell pepper, seeded and cut in slices

1 clove garlic, minced

½ teaspoon salt

4 large eggs (shells rinsed)

1 avocado, sliced

1 tablespoon tamari

Optional: Sriracha or hot sauce

Optional: One pound of top round beef, thinly sliced

Directions:

1. In medium saucepan bring 2 cups water and 1 cup rice to a boil over high heat. Lower heat to simmer. Cover. Cook until water is absorbed, 20 to 30 minutes. Set aside.

2. Heat 1½ tablespoons of olive oil in a large frying pan over medium heat. Add kale or spinach, bell pepper, garlic, and salt. Cook until kale is wilted, three to five minutes. Remove vegetables from pan and set aside. Keep warm.

3. Add remaining olive oil to same pan and fry eggs the way you like them.

4. Divide rice into four bowls and top with vegetables, eggs, and avocado. Drizzle lightly with soy sauce. Add Sriracha or hot sauce to taste.

Health Tip 101: *Eggs contain good sources of folate, protein, and choline. All of these nutrients are very important in maintaining nerve health and brain function.*

Stuffed Portobello Mushrooms

Portobello mushroom caps make attractive "bowls" for this scrumptious combination of onion, garlic, bacon, and seafood. These are special enough for when company comes over, but don't wait for an occasion to make these for yourself. Stuffed mushrooms, covered, keep in the refrigerator for one day.

Targeted Side Effect: Fatigue

Calories: 110; Total Fat: 5 g; Saturated Fat: 1 g; Total Carbohydrates: 7 g; Fiber: 2 g; Protein: 10 g

Makes 4 servings

Ingredients:

4 large portobello mushrooms

2 tablespoons olive oil, divided

3 slices non-nitrate, non-nitrite, no hormone bacon

1 large shallot or small yellow onion, chopped

3 cloves garlic, minced

6 ounces small shrimp cut in half, lump crab meat, or canned light tuna in water

⅓ cup cilantro, chopped

⅓ cup baby spinach, roughly chopped

Iodized salt and pepper, to taste

Optional: ½ cup nondairy, non-soy mozzarella cheese, shredded (we prefer Daiya)

Directions:

Preheat oven to 375°F

1. Wash mushrooms. Remove stems and chop them finely. Set aside.

2. Using ¾ tablespoon of olive oil, brush all mushroom caps on both sides with oil. Arrange stem side up on cookie sheet or baking dish. Bake for 15 minutes.

3. While the mushrooms are baking, cook slices of bacon in a frying pan over medium heat. Remove cooked bacon and set aside on paper towels to drain grease. When cool enough to handle, crumble bacon and set aside.

4. Remove grease from frying pan. Add remaining olive oil, chopped shallot or onion, garlic, and chopped mushroom stems to pan. Cook for four minutes. Add shrimp, crab, or tuna, chopped cilantro, spinach, salt, and pepper. Stir, and cook until spinach is wilted and other ingredients are blended, about three minutes. Add crumbled bacon to mixture.

5. Remove mushrooms from oven. If there is liquid in the mushrooms after baking, soak up excess water with a paper towel. Scoop out more of the mushroom around the stem to make room for filling.

6. Spoon filling into the mushroom caps and put back in the oven for 15 minutes. Serve hot.

Optional: Sprinkle with cheese, turn oven down to 350°F and cook in oven for 10 more minutes, until hot and cheese is melted.

Health Tip 101: *Portobello mushrooms are a good source of protein and contain beta-glucan, a beneficial nutrient that boosts the immune system.*

Artichoke, Bean, Hazelnut, and Asparagus Salad*

We love the satisfying crunchiness and zippy, tangy flavor of this salad.

Targeted Side Effects: Hot flashes/night sweats, fatigue, chemo brain

A good source of vitamins A and C, calcium, and iron

Calories: 230; Total Fat: 17 g; Saturated Fat: 1 g; Total Carbohydrates: 17 g; Fiber: 7 g; Protein: 7 g

Makes 6 servings
Ingredients:

1 clove garlic, minced

1 tablespoon lemon juice

½ teaspoon dried oregano

¼ teaspoon pepper

1 (14-ounce) jar artichoke hearts, quartered, in oil

1 cup cooked and drained white beans or chickpeas

¼ teaspoon salt

1 pound medium asparagus, cut into thirds, tough ends snapped off and saved for soup or discarded.

¼ cup nondairy, non-soy mozzarella cheese, shredded (we prefer Daiya)

1 cup chopped raw hazelnuts

Directions:

1. In a salad bowl, combine garlic, lemon juice, oregano, and pepper.

2. Add artichokes with their oil and beans. Toss gently.

3. In a frying pan, add salt to 1 inch of water and bring to a boil. Add asparagus, cover, and cook for three minutes or until crisp-tender.

4. Using a colander, drain asparagus and rinse under cold water. Add asparagus to salad bowl and mix well.

5. Sprinkle shredded cheese and chopped hazelnuts over salad and serve.

*This recipe is not recommended for patients on a low-fiber diet.

Health Tip 101: *Artichokes, high in flavonoid compounds, help to improve digestion by increasing bile flow and promoting optimal liver health.*

There is no medicine like hope, no incentive so great, and no tonic so powerful as expectation of something tomorrow.

———*Orison Swett Marden*

DINNER

Cod with Basil Sauce

Chili Paste Salmon

Turkey Meatloaf

Steak and Vegetable Fajitas

Coconut Fish Curry

Lentil Loaf

Pasta and Sardines

Turkey Florentine

Dahl with Spices

Shrimp Casserole

Seafood Stew

Eloise's Creole Gumbo

Eloise's Turkey and Dumplings

Grilled Halibut with Orange Ginger Sauce

Sweet and Sour Baked Chicken

Stuffed Peppers

Hot and Sour Soup with Mushrooms

Chicken with Apricots and Chickpeas

Y ou've reached the end of the day. Now is the time when you can breathe, relax, and break "bread" with loved ones. It is the meal most traditionally associated with coming together and the security of family. Sometimes we simply need the comfort dinner provides at the end of the day.

Dinner is a meal that replenishes glycogen stores in the liver and prepares you for the overnight fast.

Dinner promotes good sleep. Deep sleep is essential to healing and immune defense. During sleep you produce important antibodies and cytokines necessary to ward off infections and also to build immunity. You also produce growth hormone. In adults, the primary purpose of growth hormone is to promote repair and restoration of tissues. It helps to restore blood counts that may have taken a hit with chemotherapy and radiation.

Dinners, traditionally, have been on the heavy side, but during treatment we recommend meals high in nutrient content but light in calories to promote stable weight and to decrease symptoms associated with digestive complaints. Team these main entrees with one of our side dishes to round out your meal.

My relationship with food changed after my breast cancer diagnosis, and with the more I read and learned about the effects of my diet and cancer. I became more aware of the source and origin of the foods I purchase and consume; I read labels more; I choose organic more often; I limit my intake of fried foods, red meat, and sugar. I enjoy fruits and vegetables as a snack and substitute whole wheat and grain wherever possible. "Eating clean" is my new focus.

—K. Carhee

Cod with Basil Sauce

Basil infuses a very mild and comforting flavor to this dish. It pairs well with brown basmati rice and Roasted Brussels Sprouts with Garlic Sauce (page 74). Leftovers will keep in the refrigerator for several days and can be warmed on the stove with the sauce.

Targeted Side Effects: Fatigue, joint pain, hot flashes/night sweats

Calories: 160; Total Fat: 7 g; Saturated Fat: 1 g; Total Carbohydrate: 1 g; Fiber: 0 g; Protein: 23 g

Makes 4 servings

Ingredients:

⅓ cup fresh basil, minced

⅓ cup chicken broth

5 teaspoons olive oil, plus extra to coat pan

⅜ teaspoon sea salt, divided

2 cloves garlic, minced

4 (5-ounce) cod fillets

⅛ teaspoon black pepper

Directions:

1. In a small bowl, combine basil, broth, oil, ¼ teaspoon of salt, and minced garlic.

2. Sprinkle fish with remaining salt and pepper.

3. Coat a large pan with oil and heat over medium-high heat.

4. Sauté fish for five minutes on each side or until it flakes easily with a fork.

5. To serve, spoon basil sauce over fish.

Health Tip 101: *Basil contains anti-inflammatory nutrients and is rich in antioxidants that help protect the liver, brain, and heart.*

Chili Paste Salmon

This is a Thai-inspired dish we turn to again and again. Not only is it easy to make with minimal fuss, but it is packed with several very nutritious and beneficial ingredients, including salmon, coconut milk, and fennel. Leftovers make an excellent lunch the next day. Serve over brown rice, quinoa, or another whole grain.

Targeted Side Effects: Fatigue, nausea, gas and bloating, blood sugar regulation, anemia

A good source of vitamin C and iron

Calories: 390; Total Fat: 24 g; Saturated Fat: 18 g; Total Carbohydrates: 7 g; Fiber: 6 g; Protein: 36 g

Makes 5 servings

Ingredients:

1 fresh fennel bulb, sliced

5 (5-ounce) pieces of salmon

1 lemon, juiced

2 to 4 tablespoons of chili paste

1 cup chopped cilantro

1 (13.6-oz.) can of regular coconut milk (we prefer Westbrae)

Directions:

Preheat oven to 375°F

1. Line a large frying pan with sliced fresh fennel.

2. Arrange salmon on top of fennel, skin side down, and drizzle with lemon juice.

3. Spread a layer of chili paste on top of the fish, followed by the cilantro.

4. Pour coconut milk over the ingredients in the pan.

5. Cook the fish uncovered over low heat for 20 to 25 minutes or until fish flakes easily with a fork.

Health Tip 101: *Fennel is a carminative herb that decreases gas and bloating after eating.*

Turkey Meatloaf

This turkey meatloaf is even better the next day in sandwiches or crumbled on top of a salad. It freezes well for up to three weeks and keeps in the refrigerator for several days, so it's easy to get more than one meal from it.

Targeted Side Effects: Fatigue, anemia, insomnia, muscle aches

A good source of vitamins C and A and iron

Calories: 160; Total Fat: 3 g; Saturated Fat: 0 g; Total Carbohydrates: 13 g; Fiber: 2 g; Protein: 21 g

Makes 8 servings

Ingredients:

1 pound ground turkey

1 egg (shell rinsed), beaten

1 small to medium carrot, shredded

⅓ cup oats or gluten-free bread crumbs

½ cup sliced, sautéed mushrooms (fresh preferred but canned, drained okay)

¼ teaspoon dried oregano

¼ teaspoon dried basil or 1 tablespoon chopped fresh basil

¼ cup chopped onion

Salt and pepper, to taste

½ cup marinara sauce

Directions:

Preheat oven to 350°F

1. In a medium bowl, combine all ingredients except marinara sauce.

2. Pat into a 9 × 5-inch loaf pan.

3. Bake, covered, for 25 minutes.

4. Remove from oven and coat top of meatloaf with marinara sauce. Replace cover and bake for another 20 minutes or until the internal temperature rises to 165°F. The sauce should have thickened; If not, turn the oven to broil and broil, uncovered, for two to three minutes.

5. Be careful not to over bake or loaf will be dry.

Health Tip 101: *Turkey is a good source of protein, iron, zinc, potassium, and phosphorus. It also contains the amino acid tryptophan, which is used by the body to produce the neurotransmitter serotonin. Boosting serotonin levels can improve mood.*

Steak and Vegetable Fajitas

This healthier version of the classic Tex Mex favorite delivers on flavor and makes a hearty meal. Serve sizzling hot!

Targeted Side Effects: Fatigue, anemia, chemo brain, peripheral neuropathy

A good source of vitamin C and iron

Calories: 350; Total Fat: 16 g; Saturated Fat: 6 g; Total Carbohydrates: 25 g; Fiber: 4 g; Protein: 26 g

Makes 4 servings
Ingredients:

4 large or 8 small corn tortillas

¾ pound skirt or flank steak, cut in thin slices

¼ teaspoon kosher salt

Pepper, to taste

1 tablespoon olive oil, divided

1 medium yellow or white onion, sliced

1 bell pepper (red, green, orange, or yellow), sliced into thin strips

1 medium tomato, diced

½ cup chopped cilantro, no stems

4 tablespoons nondairy, non-soy cheddar cheese, shredded

Optional: ¼ cup nondairy sour cream

Optional: Hot sauce or salsa

Directions:

Preheat oven to 275°F

1. Heat a pan large enough to hold the tortillas on the stove over low heat. Lay a tortilla in pan, heat through, and flip over to warm the other side. Transfer to a sheet of aluminum foil. Continue stacking tortillas until all have been heated. Wrap tortillas in aluminum foil and place in warm oven.

2. Heat ½ tablespoon olive oil in a large frying pan over medium heat. Add steak and season with salt and pepper.

3. Add a tablespoon of water to pan, cover, and cook over medium heat for three minutes on each side or until desired doneness. Remove from pan, cover, and place in warm oven with tortillas.

4. To the same frying pan, pour remaining olive oil and heat over medium heat. Add onions, peppers, and salt. Cook for four minutes, stirring often. Add tomatoes and cook until softened but not mushy, about one minute.

5. Take steak out of the oven. Cut into thin slices, across meat grain. Stir into pan with vegetables. Heat through.

6. Take tortillas out of the oven. Spoon meat and vegetable mixture onto warm tortillas and top each one with chopped cilantro and shredded cheese. Serve immediately with sour cream, hot sauce, or salsa, if desired.

Health Tips 101: *Peppers contain an array of phytonutrients rich in antioxidants and vitamin C. These nutrients help to keep the immune system strong and allow it to rebound after treatment. Peppers also contain vitamin E, helpful in skin repair and hair growth.*

Coconut Fish Curry

This recipe is zesty without being overpowering. Serve over brown rice.

....

Targeted Side Effects: Fatigue, chemo brain, constipation, joint pain, peripheral neuropathy

High in vitamins A and C and iron

Calories: 330; Total Fat: 21 g; Saturated Fat: 13 g; Total Carbohydrates: 10 g; Fiber: 2 g; Protein: 26 g

....

Makes 6 servings

Ingredients:

1 tablespoon olive oil or coconut oil

1 white onion or 2 green onions, chopped

1 (13.5-ounce) can regular coconut milk

2 tablespoons tamari plus more to taste

1 teaspoon grated fresh ginger

1½ teaspoons curry powder

½ teaspoon agave syrup

6 (4-ounce pieces) whitefish (rockfish, flounder, or halibut work well)

1 (14.5-ounce) can stewed tomatoes

4 ounces cremini mushrooms, sliced

1 bell pepper, cut into strips

4 cups leafy greens, torn apart or sliced in ribbons

¼ cup chopped fresh basil or cilantro

Optional: Hot sauce

Directions:

1. Heat oil in a large pan or wok over medium heat. Add the onion and cook until slightly soft.

2. Stir in the coconut milk, tamari, ginger, agave, and curry powder. Simmer uncovered.

3. When sauce starts to bubble, add the fish, tomatoes, mushrooms, and pepper and cook, covered, for five minutes.

4. Add leafy greens and basil or cilantro. Cook until the veggies are tender. Add more tamari, if desired.

Health Tip 101: *Coconut oil contains medium-chain triglycerides, a dietary fat that offers many health benefits including acting as a quick energy source and fuel for the regeneration of gut cells. When coconut oil is digested by the body it forms monolaurin and lauric acid, two chemicals that kill harmful bacteria in the gut.*

Lentil Loaf

This delicious, earthy meal is filling and satisfying. Use slices to make a great sandwich. Keeps well in the freezer for up to two weeks.

Targeted Side Effects: Fatigue, fat metabolism

A good source of iron

Calories: 220; Total Fat: 3.5 g; Saturated Fat: 0 g; Total Carbohydrates: 36 g; Fiber: 6 g; Protein: 13 g

Makes 6 servings
Ingredients:

1½ cups dried red lentils, rinsed and debris removed

2¾ cups water or vegetable broth

½ teaspoon sea salt, plus more to taste

½ cup canned, fresh, or frozen corn kernels

⅓ cup salsa

½ cup gluten-free bread crumbs

¼ cup uncooked rolled oatmeal

2 tablespoons finely chopped cilantro

1 egg (shell rinsed), beaten

½ cup ketchup

3 ounces tomato paste

1 tablespoon olive oil

Pepper, to taste

Optional: ⅓ cup pepper slices, sautéed

Optional: ⅓ cup chopped onions, sautéed

Optional: ⅓ cup chopped garlic,

Directions:

Preheat oven to 375°F

1. In a medium saucepan, bring water or broth and lentils to a low boil. Reduce heat and simmer, covered, until liquid is absorbed, about 20 minutes. Lentils will be softened but not fully cooked. Season with salt.

2. In a large bowl, add corn, salsa, bread crumbs, oatmeal, egg, cilantro, cooked lentils, and any additional sautéed vegetables, mashing the lentils as you mix. Add salt and pepper to taste.

3. Grease 9 × 5-inch loaf pan with olive oil. Pat lentil mixture into pan. Cover with foil and bake for 30 minutes.

4. In a small bowl, combine ketchup and tomato paste. Spread over top of lentil loaf, cover with foil, and bake for 15 minutes or until a toothpick comes out clean.

Health Tip 101: *Lentils are high in protein, known to accelerate muscle regeneration. The dietary fiber found in lentils helps regulate blood sugar.*

Pasta and Sardines

This recipe is adapted from Pasta, Sardines, Bread Crumbs and Capers published in the March 26, 2010 issue of the Dining and Wine section of The New York Times. *Don't be skittish about cooking with sardines. They are inexpensive, sustainable, full of healthy omega-3 fatty acids, easy to prepare—and delicious!*

....

Targeted Side Effects: Fatigue, hot flashes/night sweats

High in vitamin C and iron and a good source of vitamin A and calcium.

Calories: 430; Fat: 17 g; Saturated Fat: 2.5 g; Total Carbohydrates: 59 g; Fiber: 4 g; Protein: 10 g

....

Makes 2 servings

Ingredients:

1½ tablespoons olive oil (you can use olive oil from the sardines), divided

1 clove garlic, minced or ½ yellow onion, chopped

¼ cup gluten-free bread crumbs

4 ounces uncooked gluten-free pasta (such as rice or quinoa pasta)

2 teaspoons lemon juice

2 (3.75-ounce) cans of skinless and boneless sardines in olive oil, drained and chopped into small pieces

¼ cup of chopped fresh parsley or 2 teaspoons dried parsley

Sea salt and pepper, to taste

Directions:

1. Heat ¾ tablespoon olive oil in medium skillet over medium-low heat. Add garlic or onion, salt, and pepper and sauté till fragrant.

2. Add remaining oil and bread crumbs to pan, stirring frequently until golden.

3. Bring a large pot of salted water to a boil and cook pasta according to directions on package until al dente. Drain, reserving a few tablespoons of cooking water.

4. To the bread crumb mixture in the skillet, add sardines, stirring frequently until mixture is heated through, about two minutes.

5. Add cooked pasta and some water to moisten and stir well to combine. Drizzle lemon juice over mixture. Season with salt and pepper to taste and garnish with parsley.

Health Tip 101: *Sardines are a good source of selenium, vitamin D, calcium, and phosphorus and are high in vitamin B12, a nutrient essential for the creation of red blood cells.*

Turkey Florentine

Susan's Aunt Gloria served this dish to her many years ago, and since then it's become a staple of her kitchen. Robust and easy to prepare, it provides a complete meal on one plate. The cooking term Florentine *can refer to any recipe that uses spinach as one of the ingredients.*

....

Targeted Side Effects: Fatigue, insomnia, blood sugar regulation

High in vitamin A, iron, and calcium and a good source of vitamin C.

Calories: 390; Total Fat: 11 g; Saturated Fat: 2 g; Total Carbohydrates: 41 g; Fiber: 2 g; Protein: 32 g

....

Makes 6 servings
Ingredients:

1 tablespoon olive oil

2 cloves garlic, chopped

2 skinless and boneless turkey breasts (about 1½ pounds total), cut into 6 pieces

20 ounces marinara sauce

1 teaspoon dried basil

1 teaspoon dried oregano

1 (6-ounce) bag fresh baby spinach or any other green leafy vegetable

3 tablespoons shredded nondairy, non-soy mozzarella cheese (we prefer Daiya)

4 ounces cooked gluten-free pasta

Salt and pepper to taste

Optional: 4 mushrooms, sliced

Directions:

1. Heat olive oil in a large skillet over medium-high heat. Add garlic and turkey pieces. Sear turkey pieces on one side, and turn over as turkey begins to turn white. Sear other side.

2. Add marinara sauce, herbs, mushrooms, if using, salt, and pepper. Cover, cook on medium-low for 10 minutes, stirring occasionally. Reduce heat to low and continue to cook, covered, until turkey is cooked through and center is no longer pink.

3. Add spinach. Cook, covered, for three more minutes, until greens wilt.

4. Top with cheese and cook until melted. Serve immediately over pasta.

Health Tip 101: *Turkey is a good source of lysine. Lysine, an essential amino acid, plays an important role in converting fatty acids into energy, a process often disturbed by steroids.*

Dahl with Spices

Always salt lentils after they are cooked. Salting them raw tends to make them tough. Store leftovers in refrigerator for up to four days. Serve with Kale Salad (page 26).

Targeted Side Effects: Fatigue, anemia

High in vitamin A and vitamin C and a good source of iron

Calories: 210; Total Fat: 9 g; Saturated Fat: 1 g; Total Carbohydrates: 25 g; Fiber: 6 g; Protein: 9 g

Makes 8 servings

Ingredients:

1 cup lentils, yellow, red, or green, rinsed and debris removed

2 cups water

1½ teaspoons sea salt

⅓ cup olive oil, plus more if needed

3 small onions, chopped

6 cloves garlic, chopped

1 tablespoon ground cumin

½ teaspoon ground ginger

½ tablespoon ground coriander

18 ounces stewed tomatoes, tomato sauce, or tomato puree

2 carrots, shredded

2 tablespoons lemon or lime juice

3 sprigs of parsley

Optional: ½ tablespoon mustard seeds

Optional: Red pepper flakes, to taste

Directions:

1. In a medium saucepan, bring water and lentils to a low boil. Reduce heat and simmer, covered, until liquid is absorbed and lentils are soft, about 30 minutes. Season cooked lentils with salt.

2. In a large frying pan, heat oil over medium heat. Add onions, garlic, and cumin. Stir frequently. Add a little more oil if ingredients stick to pan.

3. When the onions are translucent, stir in cooked lentils, other spices, tomatoes, carrots, and mustard seeds and red pepper flakes, if using. Simmer over low heat for five minutes, until mixture has melded. Stir in lemon or lime juice. Serve in bowls and garnish with parsley.

Health Tip 101: *The fiber found in lentils helps to regulate and stabilize blood sugar. Lentils are high in protein.*

Shrimp Casserole

Shrimp is high in selenium, a powerful antioxidant not found in many foods, and it's anti-inflammatory. This dish goes well with our Artichoke, Bean, and Hazelnut Salad (page 40). Saves in the refrigerator for one day.

....

Targeted Side Effects: Fatigue, chemo brain, hot flashes/night sweats, peripheral neuropathy

A good source of iron

Calories: 310; Total Fat: 12 g; Saturated Fat: 5 g; Total Carbohydrates: 26 g; Fiber: 1 g; Protein: 24 g

....

Equipment:
Ovenproof casserole dish.

Makes 4 servings

Ingredients:

1½ tablespoons olive oil, divided

3 garlic cloves, minced

1½ pounds shrimp, deveined and tails off

1½ tablespoons nondairy, non-soy margarine (we prefer Earth Balance)

⅛ teaspoon salt

⅛ teaspoon white or black pepper

½ cup gluten-free bread crumbs

¼ teaspoon dried oregano

¼ teaspoon dried basil

1 tablespoon lemon juice

8 ounces cooked rice, gluten-free pasta, or quinoa

Directions:

Preheat oven to 400°F

1. Heat ¾ tablespoon olive oil in ovenproof casserole dish over medium heat. Stir in minced garlic and margarine. Cook until garlic is golden or just beginning to brown.

2. Add ½ tablespoon olive oil, shrimp, salt, and pepper.

3. In a small bowl, combine bread crumbs, remaining olive oil, oregano, and basil.

4. Sprinkle lemon juice and then bread crumb mixture over shrimp. Bake for five minutes, until shrimp are pink and crumbs are browning. Serve over gluten-free pasta, rice, or quinoa.

Health Tip 101: *Oregano has strong antibacterial properties and can help fight oral thrush. It also helps maintain healthy gut motility.*

Seafood Stew

Our version of cioppino, an Italian-American dish originating in San Francisco, California, and traditionally made with the catch of the day. Our seafood suggestions emphasize choices that are known to be free from toxins. Seafood stew is a savory, filling, high-protein meal. Serve alone or with gluten-free whole grain dinner rolls (we prefer Udi's brand).

Targeted Side Effects: Fatigue, wound healing, joint pain, hot flashes/night sweats

High in vitamins A and C and iron

Calories: 270; Total Fat: 13 g; Saturated Fat: 2 g; Total Carbohydrates: 18 g; Fiber: 2 g; Protein: 15 g

Makes 6 servings

Ingredients:

1 (28-ounce) can crushed tomatoes

1 (28-ounce) can tomato puree

½ cup of chopped onion

⅛ cup olive oil

3 cloves garlic, minced

⅓ cup chopped celery, with leaves

⅓ cup chopped carrots

¼ cup chopped fresh parsley, no stems

2 teaspoons dried or 1 tablespoon fresh basil

1 teaspoon dried oregano

1 teaspoon dill weed

½ teaspoon red pepper flakes

¼ teaspoon sea salt

pepper, to taste

Optional: ⅓ cup red wine

Optional: 8-ounce bottle of clam juice

Seafood (use at least 3 from list):

½ pound salmon, wild, deboned and cubed

½ pound cod, deboned and cubed

1 dozen clams, rinsed

1 dozen mussels, cleaned and debearded

1 dozen shrimp, peeled and deveined

Directions:

1. In a large soup pot, add all ingredients except fish and shellfish, and heat to low boil. Turn down to simmer, cover, and cook for one hour.

2. 10 to 12 minutes before serving, add your seafood. Turn the heat up to medium and stir gently every two minutes. Shellfish is done when shells open (discard those that remain closed) and seafood is ready when it flakes easily.

Health Tip 101: *Seafood is high in omega-3 fatty acids. These fats are essential in wound repair, skin health, and decreasing inflammation. They also help to control hot flashes.*

Eloise's Creole Gumbo

Otherwise known as "Everything But the Kitchen Sink!" This family recipe was handed down by Dr. Price's grandmother Eloise and modified with gluten-free ingredients to make it hypoallergenic. Gumbo keeps for about three days in the refrigerator.

....

Targeted Side Effects: Constipation, blood sugar regulation, hot flashes/night sweats, joint pain

A good source of vitamins A and C

Calories: 360; Total Fat: 11 g; Saturated Fat: 3.5 g; Total Carbohydrates: 45 g; Fiber: 3 g; Protein: 20 g

....

Makes 8 servings
Ingredients:

3 tablespoons olive oil

3 tablespoons gluten-free all–purpose flour

½ pound chicken thighs

½ pound pork sausage, cut into small pieces

1 large onion, chopped

5 cloves garlic, minced

4 cups chicken stock or water

2 (8-ounce) bottles clam juice

½ pound fresh shrimp, deveined, shelled, and cut into small pieces

¼ pound fresh mussels

1 cup chopped okra

2 tomatoes, chopped

½ teaspoon kosher salt, plus more to taste

Fresh ground black pepper, to taste

1 bay leaf

½ teaspoon of gumbo filé, add more to taste

4 cups cooked brown jasmine rice

Directions:

1. Heat olive oil in a large pot over medium heat. Dredge chicken thighs through flour until well coated. Brown chicken thighs, five minutes on each side.

2. Add pork sausage and cook for 10 minutes, or until browned. Add onion and garlic and continue to cook for five minutes.

3. Add stock or water and claim juice. Cook on medium-low heat for 50 minutes, stirring occasionally. The gumbo should begin to thicken. Add more stock or water if it gets too thick.

4. Add shrimp, mussels, okra, tomatoes, salt, black pepper, and bay leaf to the pot and cook for 10 minutes.

5. Add gumbo filé to taste and simmer for two minutes. Remove bay leaf and serve over rice.

Health Tip 101: *Okra helps regulate blood sugar. The fiber in okra slows the absorption of sugars in the gut and promotes a healthy gastrointestinal tract.*

Eloise's Turkey and Dumplings

Dr. Price's grandmother made this hearty, comforting dish—a cross between a soup and a stew—on cold, rainy days. This dish keeps in the refrigerator for three to four days.

Targeted Side Effects: Fatigue, insomnia, peripheral neuropathy

A good source of vitamin A

Calories: 240; Total Fat: 0.5 g; Saturated Fat: 0 g; Total Carbohydrates: 46 g; Fiber: 3 g; Protein: 11 g

Makes 7 servings
Ingredients:

1 tablespoon olive oil

1 large onion, sliced

4 stalks of celery, with leaves, diced

1 bay leaf

5 cloves of garlic, chopped

3½ tablespoons gluten-free all-purpose flour

8 ounces cooked turkey breast, bone in, or leftover turkey pieces with bones

4 cups of turkey or chicken stock

¼ teaspoon dried sage or 1 tablespoon fresh

½ teaspoon dried thyme or 2 tablespoons fresh

¾ teaspoon dried rosemary or 1 tablespoon fresh

4 cups cooked brown jasmine rice

For the dumplings:

2 cups Pamela's Baking & Pancake mix or Bob's Red Mill Gluten-Free Pancake Mix

¼ teaspoon dried thyme or 1 tablespoon fresh, chopped

½ teaspoon dried parsley

dash of ground nutmeg

½ teaspoon of kosher salt

½ cup plain nondairy milk soured with 1 teaspoon of lemon juice to make buttermilk

Directions:

1. Heat olive oil in a large pot over medium heat. Add the onions, celery, bay leaf, garlic, flour, and turkey, including bones. Cook until vegetables and meat are browned.

2. Pour in stock and let simmer for an hour.

3. Season with sage, thyme, and rosemary and continue to simmer for an additional 30 minutes. Remove bay leaf and remove turkey from bones. Discard bones and cut turkey into bite-size pieces.

4. Meanwhile, prepare dumplings. In a large bowl, combine all dry ingredients. Slowly add buttermilk and mix lightly.

5. Bring soup to a boil. Drop heaping teaspoons of dumpling mixture into boiling soup. Cook for 10 to 15 minutes, or until a toothpick inserted into a dumpling comes out clean. If the soup is too thick, add more stock or water. Serve over rice.

Health Tip 101: *Celery is a good source of magnesium, calcium, and potassium, minerals that play a central role in regulating blood pressure. Celery also acts as a diuretic, helping to flush out excess fluid from the body.*

Grilled Halibut with Orange Ginger Sauce

One of our favorite recipes. This zingy orange ginger sauce pairs well with halibut and caramelizes nicely, adding a richness to this light meal. Serve with our Roasted Vegetables (page 71) or Cabbage Slaw with Almonds and Apples (page 66). Stores in the refrigerator for one to two days.

Targeted Side Effects: Fatigue, hot flashes/night sweats, joint pain

A good source of vitamin C

Calories: 360; Total Fat: 14 g; Saturated Fat: 8 g; Total Carbohydrates: 44 g; Fiber: 13 g; Protein: 20 g

Makes 3 servings

Ingredients:

2 oranges, juiced

2 tablespoons grated orange zest

1 tablespoon grated fresh ginger

1½ tablespoons coconut oil

3 (5-ounce) pieces of halibut, rinsed in cold water

½ sweet onion, sliced

1 clove garlic, minced

¼ pound green beans, washed and trimmed

½ tablespoon fresh dill weed, chopped, no stems, or 1 teaspoon dried

¼ teaspoon iodized salt

Pepper, to taste

½ avocado, sliced

Directions:

1. In a small bowl, combine orange juice, orange zest, and ginger. Set aside.

2. In a large pan, melt coconut oil on medium-high heat. Add halibut, cook for one minute, and turn over. Add onion slices, garlic and green beans. Sprinkle with dill weed, salt, and pepper. Cover and cook for one to two minutes.

3. Pour orange mixture over halibut and beans. Cover and cook for 8 to 10 minutes or until green beans are crisp and fish flakes easily with a fork.

4. Plate fish and top with avocado slices.

Health Tip 101: *Green beans are a good source of dietary fiber and vitamin C. Vitamin C helps maintain the body's blood vessels, preventing easy bruising and promoting wound healing.*

Sweet and Sour Baked Chicken

This healthier version of the Chinese takeout favorite has just the right amount of sweetness plus a hint of heat from the ginger. Baking allows all of the flavors to meld beautifully. Serve with brown basmati rice and Grilled Asparagus (page 70).

Targeted Side Effects: Fatigue, wound healing

A good source of vitamin C

Calories: 330; Total Fat: 8 g; Saturated Fat: 2 g; Total Carbohydrates: 46 g; Fiber: 2 g; Protein: 18 g

Makes 4 servings

Ingredients:

1 pound skinless and boneless chicken thighs or breasts, cut into quarters

2 bell peppers, cut into chunks

1 (10-ounce) can of pineapple chunks, drained, with juice reserved

cup water

3 tablespoons white or rice vinegar

1 tablespoon tamari or Bragg's Liquid Aminos

1½ tablespoons diced fresh ginger or crystallized ginger

½ cup honey or ¼ cup agave syrup and ¼ cup honey

3 tablespoons arrowroot

2 tablespoons sliced almonds

Directions:

Preheat oven to 350°F

1. Wash chicken and arrange in baking dish. Add peppers and pineapple on top and around chicken.

2. In a bowl, combine pineapple juice, water, vinegar, tamari or Bragg's, ginger, and honey or honey/agave mixture.

3. Add arrowroot to a pot. Place over medium heat and slowly add pineapple juice mixture, whisking continuously. Cook until sweet and sour sauce thickens.

4. Pour 1 cup sauce over chicken, peppers, and pineapple. Cover tightly with foil and cook for 35 to 45 minutes until chicken is done.

5. Sprinkle with almonds and serve with remaining sauce.

Health Tip 101: *Pineapple contains the enzyme bromelain, a natural anti-inflammatory. It also aids digestion.*

Stuffed Peppers

These stuffed peppers have an Italian flare with a hint of nuttiness from the cumin and quinoa. They go well with Grilled Tomatoes, (page 73).

....

Targeted Side Effects: Fatigue

A good source of vitamins A and C and iron

Calories: 260; Total Fat: 9 g; Saturated Fat: 2 g; Total Carbohydrates: 28 g; Fiber: 6 g; Protein: 16 g

....

Makes 6 servings
Ingredients:

½ tablespoon olive oil

¼ onion, minced

¾ tablespoon chopped cilantro or parsley

1 garlic clove, minced

¾ pound ground turkey meat

½ teaspoon ground cumin

2 tablespoons tomato paste

¾ cup cooked quinoa

6 large bell peppers, washed, tops cut off, and seeds removed*

½ teaspoon iodized salt

Pepper, to taste

½ cup shredded nondairy, non-soy mozzarella cheese (we prefer Daiya)

Optional: 1 cup steamed chopped greens such as spinach, Swiss chard, or kale

Directions:

Preheat oven to 400°F

1. Heat olive oil in skillet over medium heat. Add onions, cilantro or parsley, and garlic. Cook until onion is translucent.

2. Stir in ground turkey, cumin, salt, and pepper. Once turkey has released some of its juices, mix in tomato paste. Cook until turkey is well browned, five to seven minutes.

3. Once turkey is cooked, turn off the heat and stir in cooked quinoa, adding steamed greens, if using.

4. In a baking dish, arrange peppers cut side up and stuff each with the turkey mixture. Pour enough water into dish to cover the bottom. Cover tightly with aluminum foil and bake for 30 minutes.

5. Carefully remove foil and sprinkle cheese over top of peppers. Cook until cheese melts.

*Don't remove all the white sections inside. This part contains bioflavonoids, which are good for you. You can cut the white sections and push them onto the sides of the pepper.

Health Tip 101: *Garlic, an antimicrobial, helps prevent colds and flu.*

Hot and Sour Soup with Mushrooms

A simplified and healthier version of the classic, this low-fat, zingy soup will satisfy your spicy, sour cravings. Stores well in refrigerator for three days. Freezes well for three weeks.

Targeted Side Effects: Fatigue, loss of appetite

A good source of vitamins A and C and iron

Calories: 160; Total Fat: 4.5 g; Saturated Fat: 1 g; Total Carbohydrates: 19 g; Fiber: 2 g; Protein: 10 g

Makes 8 servings

Ingredients:

12 fresh shiitake mushrooms or dried shiitake mushrooms reconstituted with hot water

1 carrot, cut into matchsticks

1 (8-ounce) can bamboo shoots, liquid drained

8 ounces pork or chicken, cut into narrow strips

2 cups thinly sliced savoy or napa cabbage

1¾ cups water

4 cups vegetable or mushroom broth

¼ cup rice or white wine vinegar

¼ cup red wine vinegar

¼ cup tamari, more to taste

1 tablespoon Sriracha or chili–garlic sauce, more to taste

1 tablespoon grated fresh ginger

1 tablespoon arrowroot

1 tablespoon sesame or olive oil

4 ounces dry Thai rice noodles or soba 100% buckwheat noodles

Optional: ½ cup sliced scallions

Directions:

1. Cut mushroom caps into two to three slices. Discard stems.

2. Place mushrooms, carrots, and bamboo shoots in bottom of large soup pot. Add pork or chicken and cabbage.

3. In a large bowl, combine 1½ cups water, broth, vinegars, tamari, Sriracha or chili garlic sauce, and ginger. Add to soup pot. Cover and bring to slow boil. Reduce heat and simmer for one hour.

4. In a small bowl, whisk together arrowroot, sesame or olive oil, and remaining water. Stir into soup. Cover and cook over high heat for 10 minutes. stirring frequently. Drop in noodles and cook for 10 minutes.

5. Serve in bowls. Garnish with scallions.

Health Tip 101: *Shiitake mushrooms are high in protein, selenium, iron, and vitamin C. They also contain the nutrient lentinan, a type of beta glucan shown to help stimulate certain immune cells.*

Chicken with Apricots and Chickpeas

This recipe was adapted from Chickpea Tagine With Chicken and Apricots that appeared in the April 9, 2010 edition of The New York Times. *Tagine is a slow-cooked North African savory dish that is named after the earthenware pot in which it is cooked. We made the recipe gluten free and anti-inflammatory by using quinoa instead of bulgur, and adapted it for the slow cooker as well as the stew pot.*

....

Targeted Side Effects: Fatigue, wound healing, anemia

A good source of vitamin A and iron

Calories: 460; Total Fat: 17 g; Saturated Fat: 3 g; Total Carbohydrate: 53 g; Fiber: 9 g; Protein: 25 g

....

Makes 4 servings

Ingredients:

2 tablespoons olive oil

4 chicken thighs, skinless and boneless

1 large shallot or onion, chopped

1 tablespoon minced fresh ginger

1 tablespoon minced garlic

1 tablespoon ground cumin

½ cup chopped dried apricots (we prefer non-sulfured)

1 (14.5-ounce) can chickpeas, drained and liquid reserved

1 cup chicken broth

½ cup quinoa

¼ teaspoon sea salt

Pepper, to taste

½ cup chopped parsley

Directions:

1. Heat oil in a large pot over medium-high heat. Add chicken breasts and sauté four to five minutes on each side, until lightly browned. Remove from pan and set aside. Reduce to medium heat.

2. Add shallot or onion, ginger, garlic, cumin, and apricots with 2 tablespoons reserved liquid from chickpeas. Cook, stirring frequently, until mixture is heated through, about five minutes.

3. Add chickpeas, chicken broth, salt, and pepper and turn heat up to medium-high. When gently bubbling, return chicken to pot. Cover, reduce heat to low, and cook for 10 minutes.

4. Stir in quinoa and remaining reserved chickpea liquid. Cover and simmer until quinoa is done and the water is absorbed, 15 to 20 minutes.

5. Serve in bowls and sprinkle with chopped parsley.

To make in a slow cooker: Add all the ingredients to the slow cooker and set on high. When the food comes to a low boil, turn down to low, add ½ cup of water, cover, and let cook for two hours.

Health Tip 101: *Apricots are a very good source of elemental iron. It is easily absorbed and does not cause constipation.*

To hold nothing back in every breath is a spiritual practice.

—*Mark Nepo*

SIDE DISHES

Cabbage Slaw with Almonds and Apples

Brown Rice Festival

Baked Garnet Yams and Dried Fruit (Tzimmes)

Mary's Carrot and Raisin Salad

Grilled Asparagus

Roasted Vegetables

Papaya Salad

Grilled Tomatoes

Roasted Brussels Sprouts with Garlic Sauce

Mashed Root Vegetables with Herbs

Cucumber, Cantaloupe, and Squash Salad

Broccoli with Gomasio and Ginger

Garlic Snow Peas

Sweet and Sour Cabbage

Chop Chop Salad

Tomato, Pumpkin Seed, and Cilantro Salad

Potato Pancakes with Zucchini and Carrots

Carrot, Ginger, and Arame Salad

U se these side dishes to round out your lunch and dinner main entrees. Many contain a good source of fiber that will help to lower cholesterol and to keep your blood sugar stable. Others contain vital nutrients that are important in decreasing specific side effects.

Cabbage Slaw with Almonds and Apples

This side dish is sweet and crunchy. The lemon juice and vinegar bring out the flavors of the cabbage wonderfully. This recipe pairs well with Eloise's Salmon Patties (page 35).

Targeted Side Effects: Constipation, hot flashes/night sweats, blood sugar regulation, peripheral neuropathy

High in vitamins A and C

Calories: 210; Total Fat: 14 g; Saturated Fat: 15 g; Total Carbohydrates: 20 g; Protein: 4 g

Makes 8 servings

Ingredients:

2 tablespoons lemon juice

2 tablespoons rice vinegar

1 tablespoon agave syrup

¼ cup olive oil

½ teaspoon salt

1 napa or savoy cabbage, shredded

⅓ cup diced red onion

1 apple, diced small

⅓ cup slivered almonds

Optional: ⅓ cup chopped cilantro

Directions:

1. In a bowl, whisk together lemon juice, rice vinegar, agave, olive oil, and salt. Set dressing aside.

2. In a large bowl, combine cabbage, apple, onions, and slivered almonds. Toss with dressing. Garnish with additional slivered onions and cilantro, if desired.

Health Tip 101: *Cabbage is high in fiber and a good source of the amino acid glutamine, which can help prevent and treat peripheral neuropathy.*

Brown Rice Festival

Brown rice does not have to be boring. Add currants, walnuts, and red peppers for a lively sweet and savory side dish. In a covered container, this dish will keep in the refrigerator for up to three days.

....

Targeted Side Effects: Fatigue, constipation

A good source of vitamins A and C and iron

Calories: 330; Total Fat: 17 g; Saturated Fat: 1.5 g; Total Carbohydrates: 40 g; Fiber: 9 g; Protein: 7 g

....

Makes 4 servings

Ingredients:

2 cups brown rice, rinsed

4 cups water

½ cup currants

½ cup chopped walnuts

½ cup chopped red peppers

¾ cup chopped parsley

2 tablespoons olive oil

5 tablespoons lemon juice

Directions:

1. Combine rice and 4 cups water in large pot. Bring to a boil over high heat. Reduce heat to low, cover, and simmer for 40 minutes.

2. While the rice is still piping hot, add all other ingredients. Mix well.

3. Serve hot or at room temperature.

Health Tip 101: *Walnuts reduce the risk of heart disease by improving blood vessel elasticity and plaque accumulation. They are also high in omega-3 fatty acids.*

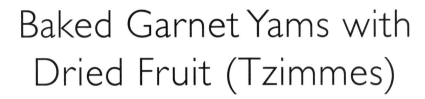

Baked Garnet Yams with Dried Fruit (Tzimmes)

Tzimmes, a Yiddish term for "big fuss," is a traditional Ashkenazi Jewish sweet stew that has become a staple at Rosh Hashanah. It is typically made from carrots and other root vegetables, often combined with dried fruits such as prunes and raisins. We chose to feature garnet yams in our version, with an assortment of dried fruit for additional vitamins, color, and natural sweetness.

Targeted Side Effects: Wound healing, anemia, loss of appetite

A good source of vitamin C and iron

Calories: 240; Total Fat: 6 g; Saturated Fat: 1.5 g; Total Carbohydrates: 47 g; Fiber: 5 g; Protein: 2 g

Makes 4 servings

Ingredients:

2 large garnet yams

2 tablespoons nondairy, non-soy margarine (we prefer Earth Balance)

½ cup dried apricots

½ cup dried cranberries

⅓ cup pitted prunes

1 tablespoon agave syrup

½ teaspoon iodized salt

Directions:

Preheat oven to 325°F

1. Place yams in medium saucepan and add water to cover. Bring to a boil, turn heat to medium, and cover. Cook until yams are easily pierced with a fork, 15 to 20 minutes.

2. Drain yams and rinse with cold water. Let cool and peel. In a bowl, mash yams with margarine.

3. In a separate bowl, combine dried fruit and agave and cover with boiling water. Let fruit sit for 15 minutes to reconstitute. Drain and chop fruit into small pieces with a knife.

4. Mix yams, fruit, and salt together. Transfer to an ovenproof dish and bake until hot, 15 minutes. Serve immediately.

Health Tip 101: *Yams are an excellent source of vitamins C and B6, both of which help maintain energy and support tissue repair and wound healing. Vitamin B6 is essential for the synthesis of red blood cells.*

Mary's Carrot and Raisin Salad

This salad, created by Dr. Price's mother, Mary, is crunchy, with a sweet, rich flavor. And it couldn't be easier to make! This salad stores in the refrigerator for about three days.

....

Targeted Side Effects: Constipation, anemia, loss of appetite, wound healing

High in vitamin A and a good source of vitamin C

Calories: 230; Total Fat: 4 g; Saturated Fat: 0 g; Total Carbohydrates: 51 g; Fiber: 6 g; Protein: 2 g

....

Makes 5 servings

Ingredients:

8 medium size carrots, grated

1 stalk celery, with leaves, chopped

2 apples, chopped

1 cup raisins

1 cup green grapes

1½ tablespoons mayonnaise or to taste

Pinch of nutmeg, to taste

Directions:

1. In a large bowl, combine all ingredients and serve.

Health Tip 101: *Apples are a good source of fiber and contain the antioxidant quercetin, which helps to stabilize histamine containing cells and may reduce the symptoms of hay fever and allergies.*

Grilled Asparagus

Asparagus is easy to make, a great addition to most meals, and a natural diuretic. Grilled with olive oil, the flavor can be described as buttery. The lemon is optional but highly recommended; a natural "brightener," it heightens the flavors in this dish.

Targeted Side Effects: Fatigue, wound healing

A good source of vitamins A and C

Calories: 100; Total Fat: 7 g; Saturated Fat: 1 g; Total Carbohydrates: 6 g; Fiber: 2 g; Protein: 3 g

Makes 2 servings

Ingredients:

1 pound asparagus

2 tablespoons olive oil

2 tablespoons balsamic vinegar

½ teaspoon chili flakes

¼ teaspoon iodized salt

Optional: Squeeze the juice of half a lemon over the top before or after cooking.

Directions:

Preheat broiler.

1. Rinse off asparagus and snap off the thick ends of the spears.
2. Spread out asparagus spears in one layer on greased cookie sheet or casserole dish.
3. Drizzle with olive oil and balsamic vinegar.
4. Sprinkle with chili flakes and salt.
5. Place under broiler for 10 minutes, turn over once, and cook for another five minutes or until asparagus are lightly browned.

Health Tip 101: *Asparagus contains the antioxidant glutathione. Glutathione is made by our bodies to fight damage done by inflammation. It is important in the restoration and repair of our tissues.*

Roasted Vegetables

Roasting vegetables condenses their flavor, making them more intense. Leaving the skin on increases the fiber content and adds nutrients. Using a variety of differently colored vegetables provides you with a range of bioflavonoids that help to keep cells healthy. Leftovers are tasty eaten cold, in a salad, or on a sandwich.

Targeted Side Effects: Fatigue, blood sugar regulation

A good source of vitamin A

Calories: 170; Total Fat: 10 g; Saturated Fat: 1.5 g; Total Carbohydrates: 19 g; Fiber: 4 g; Protein: 3 g

Makes 8 servings

Ingredients:

2 tablespoons olive oil

2 red peppers, cut into ½-inch-wide strips

1 eggplant, cut into ½-inch-thick rounds, skin on

1 sweet potato, cut into ½-inch-thick rounds, skin on

1 yellow onion, cut into ½-inch rounds

2 carrots, cut into ¼-inch rounds

1 green zucchini, cut into ¼-inch rounds

2 parsnips, cut into ½-inch-wide slices

1 yellow squash, cut into ¼-inch-round slices

1 turnip, cut into ½-inch-wide rounds

¼ teaspoon sea salt

Directions:

Preheat oven to 350°F

1. Cover cookie sheet with parchment paper.

2. With a pastry brush, coat the paper with 1 tablespoon of olive oil.

3. Arrange vegetables in one layer on cookie sheet. Brush with remaining olive oil and sprinkle with sea salt.

4. Roast in the oven, checking frequently to prevent vegetables from burning and to remove cooked, fork-tender vegetables to a covered plate to keep warm while the rest of the vegetables continue to roast.

Health Tip 101: *Red peppers are very high in vitamin C, which increases iron absorption, and a good source of vitamin B6 and magnesium, both helpful in decreasing anxiety.*

Papaya Salad

This salad was inspired by a beautiful papaya tree Dr. Price admired in West Africa. The combination of papaya, avocado, and lime will transport you to the tropics.

Targeted Side Effects: Constipation, muscle aches, joint aches, scarring, nausea

A good source of vitamins A and C

Calories: 210; Total Fat: 16g; Saturated Fat: 2.5 g; Total Carbohydrates: 18 g; Fiber: 13 g; Protein: 1 g

Makes 2 servings

Ingredients:

2 cups baby spinach

2 avocados, halved, peeled, and sliced

2 papayas, halved, peeled, and sliced

Dressing:

½ cup chopped fresh mint

1 lime, juiced

½ teaspoon salt

½ teaspoon tamari

¼ tablespoon olive oil

Directions:

1. Cover a large plate with a bed of spinach and in a line down the center, alternate papaya and avocado slices.

2. In a small bowl, whisk together mint, lime juice, salt, tamari, and olive oil.

3. Coat the spinach, papaya, and avocado with the dressing.

Health Tip 101: *Papaya, high in vitamin C and folate, contains the enzyme papain, a digestive aid.*

Grilled Tomatoes

Tomatoes are packed with nutrients including lycopene, which is proven to help reduce the chances of developing prostate cancer. Grilling them enhances their flavor, and when combined with bread crumbs and cheese, makes for a satisfying side dish or snack.

Targeted Side Effects: Fatigue, wound healing, hot flashes/night sweats

A good source of vitamins A and C and calcium

Calories: 220; Total Fat: 11 g; Saturated Fat: 2.5 g; Total Carbohydrates: 27 g; Fiber: 4 g; Protein: 3 g

Makes 2 servings

Ingredients:

2 medium to large tomatoes

Iodized salt to taste

½ cup gluten-free bread crumbs

½ teaspoon dried basil

½ teaspoon dried oregano

1 teaspoon nondairy, non-soy margarine (we prefer Earth Balance)

⅓ cup shredded nondairy cheddar cheese

Directions:

Preheat broiler.

1. Rinse tomatoes and cut in half, separating top and bottom. Remove stem. Season with salt. Arrange cut side up on a baking sheet lined with parchment paper or a lightly greased oven-safe dish.

2. In a bowl, combine bread crumbs, basil, and oregano. Sprinkle evenly over tomato halves.

3. Place ¼ teaspoon margarine on each half.

4. Place under broiler for four minutes. Tomatoes should be getting soft but not squishy, and topping should be browning but not burned. Sprinkle with cheese and broil until cheese is melted.

Health Tip 101: *Basil contains many essential oils including limonene, terpineol, eugenol, and citronellol. These oils are known to have anti-inflammatory and antibacterial properties.*

Roasted Brussels Sprouts with Garlic Sauce

When Dr. Price was a child she referred to Brussels sprouts as Martian heads. Now she just refers to them as delicious! Roasting brings out their sweetness and the garlic sauce adds a nice kick. Or skip the garlic sauce and add ⅓ cup walnut pieces and ⅓ cup dried cranberries to the Brussels sprouts when they have been roasting for 25 minutes, then continue cooking for another five minutes.

Targeted Side Effects: Hot flashes/night sweats, wound healing, fatigue, constipation

A good source of vitamins A and C and iron

Calories: 180; Total Fat: 14 g; Saturated Fat: 2 g; Total Carbohydrates: 12 g; Fiber: 4 g; Protein: 4 g

Makes 4 servings

Ingredients:

1 pound Brussels sprouts, trimmed and quartered, fresh or frozen

¼ cup olive oil, divided

¾ teaspoon iodized salt, divided

¼ teaspoon pepper

1 teaspoon lemon juice

12 garlic cloves, separated and unpeeled

Health Tip 101: *Brussels sprouts contain very high levels of vitamin C, which helps to fight infections. Vitamin C also promotes wound healing and decreases scarring.*

Directions:

Preheat oven to 400°F

1. Toss Brussels sprouts with 3 tablespoons oil, ½ teaspoon salt, and the pepper. Arrange on a baking sheet lined with parchment paper.

2. Roast for about 30 minutes or until Brussels sprouts start to brown.

3. While Brussels sprouts are roasting, make the garlic sauce. Toss garlic cloves with half the remaining oil to coat them. Wrap in aluminum foil and cook on baking sheet for 20 minutes, until squishy to the touch. When garlic is cool enough to touch, squeeze pulp out of the skins and mash with a fork. Stir in remaining oil, salt, and lemon juice.

4. Spread over Brussels sprouts and roast for an additional five minutes.

Mashed Root Vegetables with Herbs

Move over potatoes and make some room for other mashed vegetables! These enhanced mashed potatoes provide more nutrients than solo potatoes and are absolutely delicious.

Targeted Side Effects: Fatigue, wound healing, blood sugar regulation, constipation, loss of appetite

A good source of vitamins A and C

Calories: 230; Total Fat: 10 g; Saturated Fat: 3 g; Total Carbohydrates: 28 g; Fiber: 4 g; Protein: 12 g

Makes 6 servings

Ingredients:

2 Yukon gold or red potatoes, chopped into bite-size pieces, skin on

1 sweet potato, chopped into bite-size pieces, skin on

1 rutabaga, peeled and chopped into bite-size pieces

1 parsnip, peeled and chopped into bite-size pieces

1 carrot, peeled and chopped into bite-size pieces

1 beet, peeled and chopped into bite-size pieces

1 onion, chopped into bite-size pieces

1 cup chopped squash or cauliflower florets

½ teaspoon salt

4 cloves garlic, minced

1 tablespoon olive oil or nondairy, non-soy margarine (we prefer Earth Balance)

⅓ cup reserved cooking water or plain nondairy milk

1 teaspoon of whatever herbs you like, such as dill weed, paprika, turmeric, or cumin

Directions:

1. In a medium pot, cover all vegetables with water, add salt and garlic and bring to a boil. Reduce heat to simmer and cook until vegetables are fork-tender.

2. Remove from heat and drain, reserving ⅓ cup of cooking water (if you will be using).

3. Add olive oil or margarine and reserved cooking water or nondairy milk. Mash by hand or transfer to a food processor and process until smooth.

4. Season with herbs of choice and serve warm.

Health Tip 101: *Carrots and beets contain soluble fiber that helps maintain healthy gut flora and prevents and relieves constipation.*

Cucumber, Cantaloupe, and Squash Salad

Not only does this salad look fancy, it tastes delicious. It is very cooling and goes down easy.

Targeted Side Effects: Constipation, wound healing

A good source of vitamins A and C

Calories: 60; Total Fat: 3 g; Saturated Fat: 0 g; Total Carbohydrates: 8 g; Fiber: 2 g; Protein: 2 g

Makes 4 servings

Ingredients:

3 yellow summer squashes and/or green zucchini

1 cucumber, peeled

¼ large cantaloupe, rind removed

1½ cups rice wine vinegar

1 teaspoon iodized salt

Dressing:

1 cup plain nondairy yogurt

1 tablespoon lemon or lime juice

½ teaspoon kosher salt

¼ teaspoon ground cumin

¼ teaspoon pepper

Directions:

1. In a small bowl, mix dressing ingredients. Set aside.

2. Using a vegetable peeler, shave squash and cucumber into wide ribbons, excluding seeds. Place in a colander and toss with vinegar and salt. Allow the squash and cucumbers to drain for 20 to 30 minutes. Pat dry with paper towels to remove excess moisture.

3. Shave cantaloupe into ribbons and combine with drained squash and cucumber.

4. Drizzle with dressing and serve immediately or chill before serving.

Health Tip 101: *Squash is a good source of vitamin A, which promotes proper wound and tissue repair.*

Broccoli with Gomasio and Ginger

Gomasio is a traditional Japanese condiment of organic sesame seeds, seaweed, and sea salt. Paired with ginger, it adds a nice zip to the broccoli. This works well with Turkey Meatloaf (page 45).

Targeted Side Effects: Hot flashes/night sweats, nausea, muscle aches, joint aches

A good source of vitamins C and A

Calories: 70; Total Fat: 1.5 g; Saturated Fat: 0 g; Total Carbohydrates: 11 g; Fiber: 4 g; Protein: 4 g

Makes 4 servings

Ingredients:

1 large head broccoli

3 cloves garlic, minced

1 tablespoon grated fresh ginger

1 tablespoon gomasio (or 1 tablespoon sesame seeds and ¼ teaspoon sea salt)

Directions:

1. Rinse broccoli and cut into florets. Peel stems and cut into rounds.

2. Fill a pot with 2 inches of water, add broccoli and garlic, cover, and bring to a boil. When broccoli turns bright green, drain and rinse with cold water. Put back in pot and cover to keep warm.

3. In a large bowl, combine ginger and gomasio. Add broccoli and toss.

Health Tip 101: *Ginger is an excellent anti-inflammatory and relieves nausea.*

Garlic Snow Peas

Quick to make and packed with pleasing flavor, this is a great side or snack. Garlic is a good antimicrobial and helps to keep arteries flexible.

....

Targeted Side Effects: Fatigue, constipation

High in vitamin C

Calories: 100; Total Fat: 7 g; Saturated Fat: 1 g; Total Carbohydrates: 8 g; Fiber: 1 g; Protein: 2 g

....

Makes 4 servings

Ingredients:

2 tablespoons sesame oil

2 cups fresh snow peas, trimmed

3 garlic cloves, minced

Sea salt and pepper, to taste

Directions:

1. Heat wok over medium-high heat.

2. Add oil and peas.

3. Stir-fry for one minute and then add garlic, sea salt, and pepper. Peas are done when bright green and still crisp.

4. Remove from wok and serve while still hot.

Health Tip 101: *Snow peas are high in fiber, which promotes proper bowel function, and vitamins A and C.*

Sweet and Sour Cabbage

This Chinese-inspired dish uses savoy or napa cabbage, which are much easier to digest than other varieties.

Targeted Side Effects: Nausea, constipation, blood sugar regulation, loss of appetite, peripheral neuropathy

A good source of vitamins A and C

Calories: 230; Total Fat: 10 g; Saturated Fat: 1.5 g; Total Carbohydrates: 18 g; Fiber: 5 g; Protein: 9 g

Makes 5 servings

Ingredients:

1½ pounds cabbage (napa or savoy cabbage preferred)

1 tablespoon arrowroot or cornstarch

2 tablespoons agave syrup

3 tablespoons Bragg's Liquid Aminos or tamari

3 tablespoons rice or white vinegar

3 tablespoons water

3 tablespoons olive oil

½ teaspoon salt

2 teaspoons sesame seeds

2 tablespoons sliced almonds

Optional: ¾ cup cooking sherry

Directions:

1. Cut the cabbage into quarters. Remove any hard stems. Slice the cabbage quarters crosswise from top to bottom into ½-inch strips.

2. Place arrowroot or cornstarch in a medium bowl. In a separate bowl, combine agave, Bragg's or tamari, vinegar, and water. Stir into arrowroot or cornstarch and whisk together, eliminating any lumps. Set aside.

3. Place wok or sauté pan over high heat. When hot, add oil*, salt, cut cabbage, and sesame seeds and cook for one minute, stirring constantly. Stir in arrowroot mixture. Cover and cook for one more minute. Uncover and stir until the sauce thickens.

4. Remove cover, stir in sliced almonds and sherry, if desired. Serve immediately.

*Be careful: *the oil may splatter.*

Health Tip 101: *Napa cabbage is high in vitamin C. It also contains nutrients that strengthen the eyes.*

Chop Chop Salad

The star of this dish is the creamy balsamic dressing. Covered, this keeps well in the refrigerator for two days, and it is a great addition to just about any salad.

Targeted Side Effects: Fatigue, blood sugar regulation

High in vitamins A and C

Calories: 120; Total Fat: 4.5 g; Saturated Fat: 1.5 g; Total Carbohydrates: 14 g; Fiber: 4 g; Protein: 7 g

Makes 6 servings

Ingredients:

3 cups salad greens, chopped

1 (14.5-ounce) can chickpeas, drained

3 ounces diced salami

1 red pepper, diced small

½ red onion, diced small

½ cup shredded nondairy, non-soy mozzarella cheese (we prefer Daiya)

Creamy balsamic dressing:

makes 1½ cups of dressing

3 cloves garlic, finely minced

3 tablespoons mayonnaise

1 tablespoon Dijon mustard

1 tablespoon agave syrup

1½ teaspoons sea salt

½ cup balsamic vinegar

¾ cup olive, walnut, canola, or avocado oil

Directions:

1. In a large salad bowl, combine chopped greens, chickpeas, salami, red pepper, and red onion. Mix well. Add shredded cheese and mix again.

2. To make dressing, put all ingredients except vinegar and oil into a jar and shake. Add balsamic vinegar and shake again. Pour in olive oil and shake again. You can also whisk all the ingredients in a bowl.

3. Toss salad with 12 tablespoons or ¾ cup of dressing (2 tablespoons per serving).

Health Tip 101: *Chickpeas contain high amounts of dietary fiber, helpful for preventing constipation and stabilizing blood sugar levels. They are a good source of protein and have a high iron content.*

Tomato, Pumpkin Seed, and Cilantro Salad

Pumpkin seeds add crunch to this zippy yet cooling salad. Lemon juice gives this a nice fresh flavor and may be all you need for dressing, but a simple balsamic vinegar and olive oil dressing also works well.

....

Targeted Side Effects: Fatigue, wound healing, hot flashes/night sweats, muscle aches, insomnia

A good source of vitamins A and C and iron

Calories: 90; Total Fat: 5 g; Saturated Fat: 1 g; Total Carbohydrates: 9 g; Fiber: 12 g; Protein: 5 g

....

Makes 2 servings

Ingredients:

1 head romaine lettuce, washed

1 cup tomatoes, sliced

1 cup cucumbers, sliced

½ cup artichoke hearts with water, drained

1 cup chopped cilantro

⅓ cup pumpkin seeds

1 lemon, juiced

Directions:

1. Cut up the lettuce and add to a large bowl.

2. Add tomatoes, cucumbers, artichoke hearts, and cilantro to the lettuce and toss.

3. Sprinkle with pumpkin seeds.

4. Squeeze lemon juice over the salad.

Health Tip 101: *Pumpkin seeds are high in protein. They also contain helpful amounts of the amino acid tryptophan, which induces sleep. Vitamin E in pumpkin seeds promotes mucus membrane and skin health.*

Potato Pancakes with Zucchini and Carrots

Traditionally, potato pancakes do not contain other vegetables. Adding zucchini and carrots provides extra texture, vitamins, and color. Sometimes a tradition needs a little shaking up! Wrapped in aluminum foil, these pancakes will keep in the refrigerator for up to three days and in the freezer for up to two weeks. Reheat in a 400°F oven.

Targeted Side Effects: Fatigue, constipation

A good source of vitamins A and C

Calories: 250; Total Fat: 12 g; Saturated Fat: 1.5 g; Total Carbohydrates: 29 g; Fiber: 4 g; Protein: 6 g

Makes 12 servings

Ingredients:

2 eggs (shells rinsed)

1 cup mix of grated potatoes, zucchini, and carrots, drained

1 onion, grated

¼ tablespoon kosher salt

2 teaspoons pepper (white preferred for aesthetics—no black dots)

1 tablespoon gluten-free bread crumbs

½ cup vegetable or walnut oil, divided

Optional: nondairy sour cream and applesauce

Directions:

Preheat oven to 275°F

1. In a large bowl, beat eggs. Mix in potato mixture, onion, salt, pepper, and bread crumbs.

2. In a large frying pan, heat half the oil over medium heat until oil jumps when you add a small drop of water to the pan. (*Be careful, and stand back when you test oil.*) In batches, adding more oil as needed, drop 24 heaping tablespoons of potato/veggie mixture into pan. Press to flatten. Fry until browned on both sides. Place on paper towels or paper bags to drain excess oil. Blot tops with paper towel.

3. Place cooked pancakes on cookie sheet and place in the oven to keep warm until ready to serve. Serve with sour cream and/or applesauce, if desired.

Health Tip 101: *Walnut oil contains omega-3 fatty acids and healthy monounsaturated fats. Monounsaturated fats reduce inflammation and help to control blood sugar levels. Walnut oil also contains the antioxidant ellagic acid, which helps to protect the body against free radical damage.*

Carrot, Ginger, and Arame Salad

This is a very attractive looking salad that nicely blends the sweetness of carrot with the slight saltiness of the seaweed arame. The umeboshi vinegar contributes a tangy flavor and the ginger adds a little warmth to this side dish.

Targeted Side Effects: Nausea, constipation, gas and bloating, skin damage, and hair loss

A good source of vitamins C and A

Calories: 60; Total Fat: 2 g; Saturated Fat: 0 g; Total Carbohydrates: 9 g; Fiber: 6 g; Protein: 2 g

Makes 2 servings

Ingredients:

1 cup dried arame

3 cups carrots, peeled and grated

2 teaspoons toasted sesame oil

2 tablespoons sesame seeds

2 tablespoons tamari

2 tablespoons lemon juice

2 tablespoons grated fresh ginger

2 tablespoons umeboshi vinegar (can also use apple cider vinegar)

Directions:

1. Soak the dried arame in water for five minutes and then drain.

2. In a large bowl, combine carrots and arame.

3. In a separate bowl, mix sesame oil and seeds, tamari, lemon juice, grated ginger, and vinegar.

4. Toss arame and carrots with dressing.

Health Tip 101: *Arame contains iron, iodine, calcium, and magnesium. All these minerals are important for proper metabolism. Seaweeds have been traditionally used to promote hair growth.*

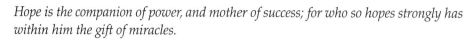

Hope is the companion of power, and mother of success; for who so hopes strongly has within him the gift of miracles.

—*Samuel Smiles*

SNACKS

Trail Mix

Spicy Roasted Chickpeas

Smoked Salmon with Cream Cheese

Quick Greens

Beet Spread with Sour Cream, Dill, and Horseradish

Hummus with Turmeric

Mushroom and Walnut Pâté

Blueberry Smoothie

Zucchini and Carrot Muffins

Green Smoothie with Probiotics

Banana Protein Shake

Snacks complement your three main meals by supplying a small amount of carbohydrates for quick energy and protein and fats for long-term energy. They keep you going throughout the day and help to maintain your metabolism and balance your blood sugar.

They also provide small doses of phytonutrients to improve mental clarity and stamina, as well as nutrients to decrease anxiety and stress.

I learned that cancer is a gift. Perhaps not one that I would have chosen for myself, but that is what makes it a gift, right? My body unlocked the very thing I needed to transform my experience of living and of loving and trusting and accepting myself and others.

—Brandi Chase

Trail Mix

Our trail mix is low in fat and includes ingredients to give you quick energy and longer lasting energy. A handful will curb your hunger and help to keep your blood sugar steady. Use waxed paper bags or a small reusable BPA-free container to carry this healthy snack with you. Store in an airtight glass container in a cool, dry place for up to ten days.

....

Targeted Side Effects: Fatigue

Calories: 70; Total Fat: 1.5 g; Saturated Fat: 0 g; Total Carbohydrates: 11 g; Fiber: 4 g; Protein: 4 g

....

Makes 14 servings

Ingredients:

1 cup Cheerios

1 cup mixed dried fruit:

    2 ounces chopped apricots

    2 ounces raisins

    2 ounces chopped pineapple or sliced banana

    2 ounces pitted, chopped prunes

1 cup raw nuts

1 cup gluten-free pretzels

1 cup dark chocolate chips

Directions:

1. In a large bowl, combine all ingredients.

Health Tip 101: *Prunes, high in elemental iron, promote bowel motility.*

Spicy Roasted Chickpeas

This is a zesty snack, especially if you are feeling like you need some extra protein. These are best eaten when they are cooled. They start to lose their crunch as time goes on, but they still taste good. If you have leftovers, store in the refrigerator in a tight-lidded jar for one day.

Targeted Side Effects: Fatigue, anemia, nausea

A good source of iron

Calories: 240; Total Fat: 10 g; Saturated Fat: 1 g; Total Carbohydrates: 29 g; Fiber: 7 g; Protein: 9 g

Makes 2 servings
Ingredients:

2 (15-ounce) cans chickpeas, drained, rinsed, and dried

½ teaspoon kosher salt

1 teaspoon ground cumin

¼ teaspoon ground coriander

½ teaspoon ground ginger

½ teaspoon cayenne

2 tablespoons olive oil

Directions:

Preheat oven to 425°F

1. Spread chickpeas on a baking sheet lined with parchment paper. Optional: Lightly rub beans to remove their thin skins.

2. Cook dry chickpeas in oven for 15 minutes.

3. Meanwhile, combine salt and spices in a small bowl.

4. Remove chickpeas from oven. Drizzle with oil and sprinkle with spice mixture. Toss to coat. Spread coated chickpeas evenly on the baking sheet.

5. Return chickpeas to oven for another 15 to 25 minutes, watching carefully so they are crunchy but do not burn.

Health Tip 101: *Coriander is a spice that acts as a carminative, helping to decrease gas and stomach cramping.*

Smoked Salmon with Cream Cheese

High in protein and good fats, this snack only requires the assembly of a few key ingredients. Capers are optional but recommended. Capers are the immature flower buds of the caper bush, which grows in the Mediterranean region. They pair well with fish and are rich in antioxidants. They are often sold in a briny solution, which keeps them fresh for many, many months.

Targeted Side Effects: Fatigue, wound healing, hot flashes/night sweats, joint pain

Calories: 160; Total Fat: 9 g; Saturated Fat: 0 g; Total Carbohydrates: 9 g; Fiber: 0 g; Protein: 7 g

Makes 4 servings

Ingredients:

8 tablespoons nondairy, non-soy cream cheese (we prefer Daiya)

4 ounces smoked salmon, sliced into 12 pieces

12 crackers (we prefer Mary's Gone Crackers)

Optional: Capers

Optional: Lemon slices

Directions:

1. Spread cream cheese on crackers and top with smoked salmon, capers, and a squeeze of lemon.

Health Tip 101: *Salmon, particularly the skin, is an excellent source of vitamin D. This vitamin is essential for a healthy immune system.*

Quick Greens*

Kale is one of the healthiest vegetables on the planet because of the variety of minerals and vitamins it contains, and it is a natural energy booster. Rich in minerals and easy to digest, tahini makes an excellent dressing.

....

Targeted Side Effects: Fatigue, insomnia, constipation

High in vitamins A and C

Calories: 270; Total Fat: 22 g; Saturated Fat: 30 g; Total Carbohydrates: 15 g; Fiber: 5 g; Protein: 9 g

....

Makes 1 serving
Ingredients:

6 leaves of kale, coarsely chopped, stalks removed and discarded

3 tablespoons tahini

1 clove garlic, minced

Chili flakes, to taste

Directions:

1. In a large bowl, combine all ingredients.

2. Let the mixture sit, covered and refrigerated, for 10 to 20 minutes, or until the kale is slightly wilted.

*This recipe is not recommended for patients on a low-fiber diet.

Health Tip 101: *Kale is high in vitamins A, C, and K and sulfur-containing phytonutrients, all of which are important in strengthening the immune system.*

Beet Spread with Sour Cream, Dill, and Horseradish

Inspired by Melissa Clark's Garlicky Beet Spread with Yogurt, Dill, and Horseradish, which appeared in the December 5, 2012 issue of The New York Times. We added potato for extra fiber and eliminated ingredients that cause inflammation. A rich, vibrant color, this spread is appealing to the eye and works well as a dip for gluten-free crackers, slices of cold potato, fresh cut carrots or celery, or radishes. Stores well in the refrigerator for up to four days.

Targeted Side Effects: Constipation, blood sugar regulation, anemia, fatigue

Calories: 45; Total Fat: 3.5 g; Saturated Fat: 0.5 g; Total Carbohydrates: 3 g; Fiber: 1 g; Protein: 1 g

Equipment:

Blender or food processor

Makes 2 cups or about 30 servings

Ingredients:

2 medium beets, scrubbed and trimmed (green leaves reserved*)

1 large potato, unpeeled

1 large garlic clove

½ cup shelled walnuts

1 teaspoon sea salt

2 tablespoons olive oil

1 cup nondairy sour cream

2 tablespoons lemon juice

1 teaspoon dried dill plus more to garnish

1½ teaspoons horseradish

Directions:

1. Place beets and potato in a medium saucepan. Fill with enough salted water to cover vegetables. Bring to a boil. Turn heat down and simmer for 10 minutes. Remove potato when still slightly undercooked. Beets are ready when a fork slips easily into them. Cut beets and potato into chunks.

2. In a blender or food processor, grind garlic, walnuts, and salt until fine. Add beets and potato. While blending or processing, slowly add 1 tablespoon of olive oil until mixture reaches a paste-like consistency.

3. Add sour cream, lemon juice, dill, and horse-radish. Blend until smooth. Add remaining oil to mixture as needed for desired consistency.

4. Store covered in the refrigerator for at least two hours to let the tastes come together before serving.

*Do not discard the beet greens! For another healthy side dish, sauté them in oil with garlic and/or red pepper flakes. To store raw greens, keep in the refrigerator, wrapped in a damp paper towel.

Health Tip 101: *Beets contain both soluble and insoluble fiber and thus are excellent for maintaining proper bowel function. They have also been shown to help decrease blood pressure.*

Hummus with Turmeric

Hummus, a good source of fiber and protein, is so easy to make there's no reason to buy it at the store. And you can adapt your homemade version of this velvety dip or spread to suit your taste. The more garlic the better for Dr. Price! Turmeric is the most potent anti-inflammatory spice you will find on your shelf, and here it adds a kick of flavor and a pop of color. Use this as a sandwich spread or as a dip for vegetables and crackers. Hummus keeps well in the refrigerator in a closed container for five days.

Targeted Side Effects: Fatigue, blood sugar regulation, insomnia

A good source of calcium

Calories: 70; Fat: 4.5 g; Saturated Fat: 0.5 g; Total Carbohydrates: 6 g; Fiber: 1 g; Protein: 3 g

Equipment:

Blender or food processor

Makes 16 servings

Ingredients:

1 (13.6-ounce) can chickpeas, drained, liquid reserved, divided

3 to 4 cloves garlic, slightly chopped

3 tablespoons fresh lemon juice

½ cup tahini

Handful of fresh parsley, no stems, roughly chopped

½ teaspoon dried turmeric

Salt, to taste

Optional: 3 roasted red peppers (drain liquid from jarred, reserve)

Directions:

1. In a blender or food processor, blend half the chickpeas, three-quarters of reserved liquid, and garlic until smooth. Add more liquid as needed.

2. Add lemon juice and tahini and blend until combined.

3. Add rest of chickpeas, parsley, turmeric, and red peppers, if using, and blend until smooth, occasionally scraping down sides to blend evenly. If hummus is too thick, add more reserved liquid from beans or red peppers.

Health Tip 101: *Lemons are high in vitamin C, a nutrient that helps to strengthen immune activity and decrease free radical damage. In addition, vitamin C, used by the adrenal glands, is involved in decreasing stress and promoting a relaxed state.*

Mushroom and Walnut Pâté

Mushrooms are an excellent source of the antioxidant selenium and vitamin D. This rich, moist pâté is perfect as a snack or an appetizer. Keeps well covered in the refrigerator for one week. Serve with gluten-free crackers.

Targeted Side Effects: Fatigue, anemia, wound healing

Calories: 130; Total Fat: 12 g; Saturated Fat: 2 g; Total Carbohydrates: 3 g; Fiber: 1 g; Protein: 2 g

Equipment:

Blender or food processor

Makes 16 servings

Ingredients:

1 cup walnut halves

½ cup nondairy, non-soy margarine (we prefer Earth Balance)

½ onion, chopped

¼ pound shiitake mushrooms, chopped

¼ lb. cremini mushrooms, chopped

¼ lb. portobello mushrooms, chopped

1 tablespoon roasted garlic*

¼ cup chopped fresh Italian parsley

½ teaspoon dried thyme

½ teaspoon sea salt

½ teaspoon white pepper

2 tablespoons olive oil

Directions:

Preheat oven to 350°F

1. In a small frying pan, spread walnuts in a single layer and toast over low heat for 10 minutes, or until fragrant.

2. In a large frying pan, melt margarine over medium heat. Add onion and cook until soft.

3. Mix in mushrooms, garlic, parsley, thyme, salt, and pepper, stirring until all are mixed and cooked.

4. In a blender or food processor, process walnuts and olive oil until mixture forms a thick paste. Add mushroom mixture and process until smooth.

5. Transfer to a bowl, cover with plastic wrap, and refrigerate for at least four hours, though it is best if chilled overnight.

*To roast garlic: *Toss two to three garlic cloves, separated and unpeeled, with enough olive oil to coat them. Wrap in aluminum foil and cook on baking sheet for 20 minutes until soft. When cloves are cool enough to handle, squeeze pulp out of skins.*

Health Tip 101: *Walnuts are an excellent source of vitamin E, an important antioxidant required for maintaining the health and integrity of the mucus membranes and skin.*

Blueberry Smoothie

Smoothies are a refreshing snack, and blueberries are one of the healthiest fruits you can consume. This smoothie is silky and lightly sweet. Try substituting raspberries or mixing them together.

....

Targeted Side Effects: Fatigue, constipation, loss of appetite

A good source of vitamin C, calcium, and iron

Calories: 350; Total Fat: 18 g; Saturated Fat: 3 g; Total Carbohydrates: 49 g; Fiber: 6 g; Protein: 8 g

....

Equipment:
Blender or immersion blender

Makes 1 serving
Ingredients:
½ cup almond milk or coconut water

1 banana

½ cup blueberries, fresh or frozen

1 pear, peeled, cored, and chopped

1 mango, peeled, seeded, and chopped

2 tablespoons almond or cashew butter

Directions:
1. Blend ingredients until smooth. Enjoy immediately.

Health Tip 101: *Blueberries contain chromium, a mineral shown to help stabilize blood sugar levels, particularly for patients suffering from diabetes type 2.*

Zucchini and Carrot Muffins

These muffins are moist and light. Even kids love them! They're a great way to sneak in vegetables. The muffins freeze well and can be served with margarine, jam, or nut butter, but we like them naked right out of the oven.

Targeted Side Effects: Constipation, blood sugar regulation

Calories: 80; Total Fat: 0 g; Saturated Fat: 0 g; Total Carbohydrates: 20 g; Fiber: 2 g; Protein: 0 g

Makes 12 muffins

Ingredients:

¼ cup walnut oil or olive oil

3 tablespoons agave syrup (we prefer dark)

1 egg (shell rinsed)

¾ cup unsweetened applesauce

1 cup grated carrots)

1 cup grated zucchini

1 cup Bob's Red Mill Gluten Free Biscuit and Baking Mix

¾ cup sorghum or additional Bob's Red Mill Gluten Free Biscuit and Baking Mix

2 teaspoons baking powder

1 teaspoon cinnamon

½ teaspoon iodized salt

Paper muffin cups

Directions:

Preheat oven to 400°F

1. In a large bowl, combine oil and agave. Beat in the egg. Mix in applesauce. Stir in carrots and zucchini.

2. In a medium bowl, combine flours, baking powder, cinnamon, and salt.

3. Add dry ingredients to wet and stir until just combined.

4. Divide the batter evenly among 12 paper lined muffin pan cups. Bake 12 to 16 minutes or until a toothpick stuck into the middle of one muffin comes out clean.

Health Tip 101: *Soluble fiber in apple sauce is important in absorbing water and regulating bowel movements. Soluble fiber also is helpful for maintaining proper gut microflora.*

Green Smoothie with Probiotics

Don't think a green drink can be delicious? Try this one. The mango and ginger add sweetness and spice. Kombucha tea is a fermented drink made with tea, sugar, bacteria, and yeast.

Targeted Side Effects: Constipation, hot flashes/night sweats

A good source of vitamins A and C, calcium, and iron

Calories: 110; Total Fat: 2.5 g; Saturated Fat: 2 g; Total Carbohydrates: 24 g; Fiber: 5 g; Protein: 3 g

Equipment:

Blender or immersion blender

Makes 1 serving

Ingredients:

¼ cup chopped frozen or fresh mango

¼ cup spinach, no stems

¼ small cucumber, peeled and chopped

½ tablespoon fresh parsley or cilantro, no stems

4 ounces organic kombucha tea (we prefer GT's)

¼ cup rice or coconut yogurt

½ inch fresh ginger, peeled and chopped

2 ice cubes, crushed (to crush, place cubes in plastic bag and smash with metal ladle or similar kitchen utensil)

Directions:

1. Blend mango, spinach, cucumber, parsley, kombucha, and yogurt. When well combined, add chopped ginger and crushed ice and blend until smooth.

2. Pour into glass and drink immediately.

Health Tip 101: *Kombucha contains natural probiotics helpful in replenishing gut flora. It is rich in energy boosting B vitamins.*

Banana Protein Shake

Rich and creamy, this decadent shake packs a protein punch.

Targeted Side Effects: Loss of appetite, weight loss, fatigue

A good source of vitamin C

Calories: 290; Total Fat: 25 g; Saturated Fat: 22 g; Total Carbohydrate: 17 g; Fiber: 2 g; Protein: 5 g

Equipment:

Blender or immersion blender

Makes 2 servings

Ingredients:

1 ripe banana

1 cup coconut milk

1 cup crushed ice (to crush, place cubes in plastic bag and smash with metal ladle or similar kitchen utensil)

2 tablespoons hemp, pea, or rice protein powder

Directions:

1. Blend all ingredients until smooth.

2. Pour into glasses and serve immediately.

Health Tip 101: *Bananas are a rich source of potassium, an essential nutrient for energy as well as heart and muscle health.*

Hope arouses, as nothing else can arouse, a passion for the possible.

—*William Sloan Coffin*

DESSERTS

Chocolate Covered Figs

Banana with Chocolate and Walnuts

Carob Fudge

Melon "Ice Cream"

Crispy Chewies

Balsamic Blueberries

Chocolate Pudding

Desserts do not have to contain high amounts of added sugars or trans fats to be delicious. Believe it or not, desserts can be beneficial, especially if they provide naturally occurring nutrients that are anti-inflammatory, heart healthy, and contain protein. And these desserts don't have to taste like cardboard!

Our recipes contain whole foods and fresh ingredients while still satisfying the desire for sweets.

Discover these new flavor sensations that not only taste good but are good for you.

I'm 35 years old and a cancer survivor. There are so many kind words, positivity and prayers out there. I know that being positive is difficult but you must be positive and fight harder than you ever have...Not knowing what my future held made each day special, I didn't know if I would be around the next year. That thought kept me fighting. My strength kept my family and friends strong to pray more and enjoy every day. I never thought I was being strong. But looking back I am a stronger person who is closer to God, my family, and friends.

—AM

Chocolate Covered Figs

In this treat, turmeric adds a light, peppery heat to the chocolate. You may want to add only half the turmeric and adjust to taste. Refrigerated, in a closed container, these will keep for several days—but they won't last that long!

··

Targeted Side Effects: Constipation, fatigue, anemia, blood sugar regulation

A good source of vitamin C

Calories: 170; Total Fat: 7 g; Saturated Fat: 42 g; Total Carbohydrates: 29 g; Fiber: 2 g; Protein: 2 g

··

Makes 4 servings

Ingredients:

½ cup or 4 ounces dark chocolate, broken into chunks

½ teaspoon grated orange zest

⅓ teaspoon dried turmeric

8 dried figs

Directions:

1. Line a baking sheet with waxed paper.

2. *To melt chocolate:* Use a double boiler or place chocolate in a light, nonplastic bowl over a pot of lightly steaming water. Stir constantly until chocolate is melted. Remove from water bath.

3. If you prefer, place chocolate in small microwave-safe bowl or cup. Cover with waxed paper and heat in microwave on high power for 30 second intervals or until chocolate is almost melted. Stir until smooth.

4. To the melted chocolate, add orange zest and turmeric.

5. Hold one fig by the stem and dip into melted chocolate until the bottom half is covered. Repeat with remaining figs and chocolate.

6. Set figs on prepared baking sheet until chocolate hardens. You can put the figs in the refrigerator to speed up hardening, especially if you're making this during the summer months.

Health Tip 101: *Dark chocolate contains flavonoid, an antioxidant which helps protect the body from damage. The flavonoid also aids in reducing insulin resistance by helping cells to respond to insulin appropriately. But remember, a little goes a long way.*

Banana with Chocolate and Walnuts

Don't be deceived by the paucity of the ingredients. This combination of flavors and textures yields a simple yet satisfying dessert.

Targeted Side Effects: Fatigue, wound healing

Calories: 150; Total Fat: 7 g; Saturated Fat: 3 g; Total Carbohydrates: 30 g; Fiber: 3 g; Protein: 2 g

Makes 1 serving

Ingredients:

1 tablespoon semisweet chocolate chips

½ banana, thinly sliced into rounds

½ tablespoon chopped walnuts

⅓ teaspoon dried turmeric

Optional: 1 tablespoon nondairy yogurt

Directions:

1. Place chocolate in small microwave-safe bowl or cup. Cover with waxed paper and heat in microwave on low power for 10 second intervals or until chocolate is almost melted. Stir until smooth. Stir in turmeric.

2. To serve, arrange banana rounds on a plate and sprinkle with walnuts. Serve with melted chocolate on the side for dipping or drizzle on top. Top with yogurt, if desired.

Health Tip 101: *Walnuts are a good source of protein and are rich in omega-3 fatty acids. A heart-healthy nut, walnuts are recommended for people over 50.*

Carob Fudge

If you've never tried carob, this fabulously rich fudge will be a real treat. Carob comes from the dried pod of a tree native to the eastern Mediterranean and has several advantages over cocoa: it's caffeine-free, rich in zinc, and contains three times as much calcium. When covered, fudge stores well in the refrigerator for several days.

Targeted Side Effects: Loss of appetite, blood sugar regulation

Calories: 230; Total Fat: 14 g; Saturated Fat: 2.5 g; Total Carbohydrates: 26 g; Fiber: 3 g; Protein: 5 g

Makes 18 servings

Ingredients:

½ tablespoon nondairy, non-soy margarine (we prefer Earth Balance)

1 cup agave syrup

1 cup freshly ground or smooth peanut or almond butter

1 cup carob powder

¾ cup raw sunflower seeds

½ cup chopped walnuts, more for topping if desired

Optional: ½ cup unsweetened shredded coconut

Optional: ½ cup dried cranberries, currants, or raisins

Directions:

1. Grease an 8-inch-square baking dish with margarine.

2. In a large pan over medium-low heat, combine agave and nut butter, stirring until smooth.

3. Remove from heat and stir in carob powder until well combined.

4. Mix other ingredients into carob mixture.

5. Spread evenly into baking dish, top with additional walnuts, if using, and chill uncovered in refrigerator for three hours. Cut into pieces and serve.

Health Tips 101: *Carob is high in vitamin E and calcium. It contains gallic acid, an antibacterial and antiviral.*

Melon "Ice Cream"

This light dessert is perfect during the summer, when melon is plentiful and the weather is warm.

Targeted Side Effects: Constipation, fatigue

A good source of vitamin C and A

Calories: 45; Total Fat: 0.5 g; Saturated Fat: 0.5 g; Total Carbohydrates: 9 g; Fiber: I g; Protein: I g

Equipment:
blender or immersion blender

Makes 4 servings

Ingredients:

½ honeydew or cantaloupe melon, fresh or frozen, no rind or seeds

I cup vanilla-flavored nondairy milk

I ½ cups ice, more as needed

Optional: ⅛ teaspoon ground ginger or cinnamon

Directions:

1. Blend all ingredients until smooth.

2. Serve immediately or "ice cream" will melt.

Health Tip 101: *Cantaloupe is a good source of vitamin C and soluble fiber. Vitamin C stimulates white blood cells and keeps bacteria and viruses at bay.*

Crispy Chewies

Perfect if you're craving something sweet and crunchy. A little goes a long way. Chocolate is high in zinc and helps to stimulate appetite. Refrigerated and covered, these keep for over a week.

....

Targeted Side Effects: Fatigue

Calories: 110; Total Fat: 5 g; Saturated Fat: 1 g; Total Carbohydrates: 18 g; Fiber: 3 g; Protein: 2 g

....

Makes 18 servings

Ingredients:

½ cup dark chocolate or carob chips

1 cup agave syrup

½ cup nut butter

3 cups crispy brown rice cereal

Directions:

1. In a small microwave-safe bowl or cup, combine chocolate or carob chips, agave syrup, and nut butter. Cover with waxed paper and heat in microwave on high power for 30 second intervals until chocolate is almost melted. Stir until smooth.

2. Stir in brown rice cereal.

3. Pour into shallow baking pan.

4. Let cool to room temperature and cut into pieces.

Health Tip 101: *Dark chocolate increases blood flow to the brain and promotes good feelings associated with love. Small amounts can control blood sugar by helping to reduce insulin resistance. Dark chocolate also has a low glycemic index, which means it won't spike your blood sugar levels.*

Balsamic Blueberries

This unusual blend of flavors creates a full-bodied taste sensation that will excite your palate. The flavor of the fruit is enhanced by the tang of the balsamic vinegar.

....

Targeted Side Effects: Blood sugar regulation, wound healing

A good source of vitamin C

Calories: 140; Total Fat: 0 g; Saturated Fat: 0 g; Total Carbohydrates: 35 g; Fiber: 3 g; Protein: 1 g

....

Makes 4 servings

Ingredients:

2 tablespoons agave syrup

1 tablespoon balsamic vinegar

1 cup fresh blueberries

¼ pound fresh peaches, pitted and sliced

¼ teaspoon black or white pepper

Directions:

1. In a heavy saucepan, boil agave, balsamic vinegar, and ⅓ cup blueberries, stirring constantly, for one minute. Remove from heat.

2. In a large bowl, combine the rest of the blueberries with peach slices.

3. Toss with hot blueberry syrup and pepper.

4. Let stand, stirring occasionally, to cool slightly before serving.

Health Tip 101: *Blueberries contain high amounts of chromium, an element useful in controlling blood sugar. Diabetics and pre-diabetics often will experience blood sugar elevations during chemotherapy.*

Chocolate Pudding

Goodbye to stirring over a hot stove! This sweet, super quick, and healthier version provides instant gratification.

....

Targeted Side Effects: Fatigue

A good source of calcium

Calories: 220; Total Fat: 7 g; Saturated Fat: 5 g; Total Carbohydrates: 70 g; Fiber: 5 g; Protein: 3 g

....

Makes 1 serving
Ingredients:

8 ounces coconut yogurt

⅓ cup cocoa powder

2 tablespoons agave syrup

Directions:

1. In a small bowl, mix all ingredients and stir until well combined.

Health Tip 101: *Yogurt is a good source of calcium and probiotic bacteria. Calcium not only is good for bones but it also promotes relaxation and sleep.*

There is something beautiful about all scars of whatever nature. A scar means the hurt is over, the wound is closed and healed, done with.

—*Harry Crews*

EATING AS A PRESCRIPTION

Bone Broth

Smothered Liver

Nutritional Vegetable Broth

Tuna and Avocado Salad

Mango Lassi

Nutty Smoothie

Coconut "Ice Cream"

Sometimes eating isn't appealing. Your taste buds have gone south; nothing tastes right. Your stomach is constantly revolting, and nausea is inevitable. Eating may even result in diarrhea up to 12 times a day and into the evening. As a result, you push away from food and rapid weight loss ensues. This is the point where eating needs to become a prescription. One of the most important things during cancer treatment is to maintain a stable weight. For patients who are overweight at the start of cancer treatment, a switch to a more balanced, nourishing diet may result in a slow weight loss, then stabilization.

In our experience patients who tend to have the most issues with weight loss during treatment are those diagnosed with gastrointestinal cancers. But anorexia and resulting weight loss can happen to anyone. Problems with diarrhea, nausea, and stomach upset should be stabilized by your doctor.

To stop the weight loss you should try to eat a small amount every two hours. Check with your doctor to see if this is suitable for you. Even though you don't feel like eating, think of it as taking a lifesaving pill.

The light meals in this section are high in nutrients while being easy to digest—and tasty. They are meant to stimulate your appetite so that you are able to eat more calorie-laden meals.

My diagnosis was a clarion bell. I meditated regularly, but I must confess, at that moment, for the first time in my life, I experienced clarity. At that moment, through to the apex of my treatment, anything beyond the present was meaningless. I lived in my moment by moment consciousness. What is astonishing is how, now that the crisis has passed, I can let days slip by without attention. Sometimes I think, did I learn nothing? And then I realize: no, you learned something, because you noticed.

—*Brandi Chase*

Bone Broth

This broth is dense in nutrients and minerals and easy to digest. Buy soup bones from the butcher. These bones will have very little meat on them but will be a source of bone marrow, which is the base of the nutrients in the broth. It's excellent on its own or as a soup base. Add vegetables, dumplings, or whatever you fancy. Broth keeps in the refrigerator for four to five days and in the freezer for up to two to three months. Be sure to cool to room temperature before freezing, and consider freezing in single-serve portions for an easy meal.

Targeted Side Effects: Anemia, loss of appetite, nausea, bone health, insomnia, hydration

A good source of iron and calcium

Calories: 55; Total Fat: 0 g; Saturated Fat: 0 g; TotalCarbohydrates: 11 g; Fiber: 0 g; Protein: 3 g

Makes 6 to 8 servings

Ingredients:

1.5 to 2 pounds of beef marrow bone (organic, hormone free)

4 quarts of water

1 head fresh garlic, peeled and chopped

1 cup apple cider vinegar

1 teaspoon kosher salt

2 onions, chopped

2 stalks of celery, with leaves, chopped

Directions:

Preheat oven to 375°F

1. Arrange bones on a baking sheet in a single layer and roast for 25 minutes, turning the bones halfway through the cooking time, until nicely browned.

2. In a large soup pot, add roasted bones and all the other ingredients.

3. Bring to a boil, and reduce heat to simmer for 8 to 24 hours. The longer you cook the stock, the more flavorful it will be.

4. Remove from heat, let cool, and skim off any fat that has risen to the surface. Strain the liquid and discard the bones.

Health Tips 101: *The micronutrients found in bone broth, such as zinc and manganese, help to stimulate the appetite and provide nutrients for immune cell production.*

Smothered Liver

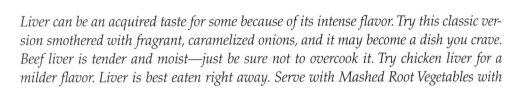

Liver can be an acquired taste for some because of its intense flavor. Try this classic version smothered with fragrant, caramelized onions, and it may become a dish you crave. Beef liver is tender and moist—just be sure not to overcook it. Try chicken liver for a milder flavor. Liver is best eaten right away. Serve with Mashed Root Vegetables with Herbs (page 75).

Targeted Side Effects: Loss of appetite, anemia, weight loss

A good source of vitamins A and C and iron

Calories: 250; Total Fat: 11 g; Saturated Fat: 2 g; Total Carbohydrates: 23 g; Fiber: 1 g; Protein: 18 g

Makes 2 servings

Ingredients:

3 tablespoons olive oil, divided

5 medium onions, sliced thin

3 tablespoons brown rice flour

1 teaspoon iodized salt

½ teaspoon black pepper

1 pound organic, hormone free, beef or chicken liver, thinly sliced

¾ cup water

Directions:

1. Heat 1 tablespoon olive oil in a large frying pan over medium heat. Add onions and sauté until translucent. Remove onions from pan and set aside.

2. While onions are sautéing, in a bowl, mix flour with salt and pepper.

3. Working in batches, dredge thinly sliced liver in the flour and transfer to a large plate.

4. Heat remaining oil over medium heat in the same frying pan used to cook onions. When pan is hot, fry liver to brown on both sides.

5. Add cooked onions and water and cover until liver is tender, 20 to 30 minutes.

Health Tip 101: *Liver is a rich source of elemental iron and vitamin B12, and both of these nutrients are necessary for red blood cell production.*

Nutritional Vegetable Broth

Drink this broth in the morning to start the day with a warm, liquid, low-calorie natural multivitamin. With its multitude of vegetables, it is very hydrating. Personalize it by adding more vegetables, noodles, rice, meat, mushrooms, tofu, or dumplings. This broth stores well in a closed container for four to five weeks in the freezer. Cool completely before storing.

Targeted Side Effects: Loss of appetite, anemia, fatigue, wound healing, bone health, joint pain, nausea, hydration

High in vitamins A and C, calcium, and iron

Makes 4 to 6 servings

Ingredients:

1½ pounds sweet onions, cubed

1 pound carrots, cubed

1 pound red and green peppers, cubed

1 pound broccoli, cut into small florets and peeled, stem cut into rounds

3 to 4 cloves garlic

2 tablespoons olive, macadamia nut, or coconut oil

1 pound of maitake mushrooms

1 pound celery, with leaves, cubed

3 to 4 tablespoons grated fresh ginger

3 to 4 tablespoons grated fresh turmeric root

1 bunch parsley, chopped

1 bunch cilantro, chopped

1 pound collard greens, chopped

1 gallon of water

Directions:

Preheat oven to 450°F

1. In a large roasting pan, toss onions, carrots, peppers, broccoli, and garlic in oil. Add mushrooms (do not toss in oil). Roast, turning every 15 minutes, until vegetables are browned, about 30 minutes.

2. Once browned, transfer vegetables to a large stockpot. Add celery, roots, parsley, cilantro, and collard greens. Pour in water.

3. Bring to full boil and then reduce heat to a simmer.

4. Simmer uncovered until the liquid is reduced by half.

5. Strain the liquid through a mesh colander, reserving stock and discarding vegetables.

Health Tip 101: *In Asia, maitake mushrooms have been used for centuries for their medicinal qualities. Polysaccharides in the mushrooms have been shown to stimulate the immune system.*

Tuna and Avocado Salad

Quick to make, easy to eat, this recipe is a good choice for patients whose appetite has gone downhill. Fresh cilantro, mustard, and lemon juice will wake up your taste buds. A sprinkle of dulse is optional but recommended. Also known as Palmaria palmata, this red seaweed is packed with minerals, including iron and potassium, and vitamin B-12.

....

Targeted Side Effects: Loss of appetite, weight loss, wound healing, fatigue

High in vitamin C

Calories: 330; Total Fat: 27 g; Saturated Fat: 4 g; Total Carbohydrates: 10 g; Fiber: 7 g; Protein: 15 g

....

Makes 2 servings

Ingredients:

1 (5-ounce) can tuna, in water

4 tablespoons mayonnaise

2 tablespoons celery, chopped

1 tablespoon parsley, chopped

1 tablespoon cilantro, chopped

1 teaspoon mustard

½ teaspoon black pepper

1 tablespoon lemon juice

1 ripe avocado

Optional: 1 teaspoon dulse granules or
flakes*

Directions:

1. In a large bowl, combine all ingredients except avocado.

2. Halve avocado. Remove pit. Place sections on a plate

3. Spoon tuna salad into avocado pieces and sprinkle with dulse. Serve immediately.

*This recipe is not recommended if your palette has altered and foods taste too salty to you.

Health Tip 101: *Parsley is an anti-inflammatory and a good source of vitamin K, necessary to maintain the myelin sheath around nerves.*

Mango Lassi

Lassi is a popular, traditional yogurt-based drink from Bangladesh, India, and Pakistan. Creamy and cool, this mouthwatering drink goes down easy. Add a hint of cardamom for added spice and warmth. Consume immediately.

....

Targeted Side Effects: Loss of appetite, weight loss, wound healing, anemia, nausea

A good source of vitamins A and C and calcium

Calories: 180; Total Fat: 6 g; Saturated Fat: 6 g; Total Carbohydrates: 68 g; Fiber: 6 g; Protein: 1 g

....

Equipment:

blender or immersion blender

Makes 2 servings

Ingredients:

2 cups nondairy yogurt (we recommend coconut or coconut–rice yogurt)

1 cup mango chunks, fresh or frozen

1 cup ice

½ cup water

Optional: ¼ teaspoon ground cardamom

Directions:

1. Blend all ingredients until smooth.

Health Tip 101: *Mangoes are a good source of vitamin E and high in iron.*

Nutty Smoothie

This delicately flavored smoothie goes down easy and stays down. Keeps well for several hours covered and refrigerated.

Targeted Side Effects: Nausea, anorexia, fatigue, constipation, insomnia

A good source of calcium

Calories: 180; Total Fat: 7 g; Saturated Fat: 0 g; Total Carbohydrates: 30 g; Fiber: 8 g; Protein: 3 g

Equipment:
Blender

Makes 2 servings

Ingredients:
1 large fresh pear, cored and chopped

½ banana

1 tablespoon almond butter

½ teaspoon hemp seeds

1 teaspoon agave syrup

1 cup cold almond milk

Optional: 2 ice cubes

Directions:
1. Combine all ingredients in blender. Pour into glasses, and add ice cubes for a cooler drink, if desired.

Health Tip 101: *Hemp seeds are high in protein and omega-6 fatty acids. Both these nutrients help to combat fatigue and tissue healing at every phase of treatment. In addition, the high content of magnesium helps to trigger the conversion of serotonin to melatonin for restful, deep sleep.*

Coconut "Ice Cream"

If you like coconut, you'll love this velvety smooth, soothing dish.

....

Targeted Side Effects: Nausea, anorexia,

A good source of iron

Calories: 280; Total Fat: 27 g; Saturated Fat: 24 g; Total Carbohydrates: 10 g; Fiber: 3 g; Protein: 3 g

....

Equipment:

Blender

Makes 1 serving

Ingredients:

1 cup almond milk

1 (14-ounce) can regular coconut milk

½ cup So Delicious Coconut Creamer

½ cup unsweetened flaked coconut (We recommend Bob's Red Mill)

Directions:

1. Blend almond and coconut milk in blender.

2. Pour into a sealable plastic or metal container. Stir in creamer and flaked coconut.

3. Freeze for two hours or until solid.

Health Tip 101: *Because almonds are so high in phosphorus, they are helpful in maintaining good bone health. This is especially important during hormone therapy, when bone loss (osteoporosis) can be a real issue.*

I have no power of miracle other than the attainment of quiet happiness, I have no tact except the exercise of gentleness.

—Oracle of Sumiyoshi

BEVERAGES

Orange-Orange Juice

Jazzy Apple Juice

Blueberry Kale Juice

Power Green Juice

Vegetable–Fruit Drink

Craneberry Tea

Staying hydrated is a vital way to stave off nausea and fatigue while undergoing cancer treatment. Juices can also be a way to get in your daily allowance of vegetables and fruits when you don't feel like eating or if you are running from appointment to appointment and don't have time. For the four juice recipes here we recommend using a juicer, which extracts only the juice of the fruit or vegetable. If you don't have a juicer, try our Vegetable–Fruit Drink and Craneberry Tea. Drink these healthful beverages in addition to eight glasses of water per day.

Orange-Orange Juice

Targeted Side Effects: Fatigue wound healing, hydration

1 medium orange, peeled and quartered

1 medium apple, cut into fourths

2 large carrots

½-inch piece fresh turmeric root, peeled

Jazzy Apple Juice

Targeted Side Effects: Fatigue, constipation, hydration

1 medium apple, cut into fourths

1 large beet

1-inch piece fresh ginger, peeled

½ lemon, peeled and halved

Pinch of cinnamon

Blueberry Kale Juice

Targeted Side Effects: Fatigue loss of appetite, hydration

3 kale leaves

1 pear, cut into fourths

1 medium apple, cut into fourths

1 cup blueberries

Power Green Juice

Targeted Side Effects: Fatigue, hydration

1 medium tomato

3 kale leaves

½ cup fresh parsley

3 cups spinach

1 large cucumber

1 medium apple, cut into fourths

Vegetable–Fruit Drink

This drink is a fantastic way to start your day or enjoy as a midday snack. Keeps well covered in the refrigerator for one day. Shake well or blend before drinking.

Targeted Side Effects: Fatigue, anemia, hydration

A good source of vitamin A and iron

Calories: 220; Total Fat: 17 g; Saturated Fat: 11 g; Total Carbohydrates: 16 g; Fiber: 3 g; Protein: 4 g

Equipment:
Blender

Makes 2 servings
Ingredients:

½ medium apple, cored and diced

Handful of Swiss chard or baby spinach, rinsed

½ cup coconut milk

½ cup vanilla almond milk

1 tablespoon creamy nut butter

½ cup sliced peaches

6 to 8 ice cubes

Directions:

1. Blend all ingredients except ice until well combined.

2. Add ice and blend until smooth.

Health Tip 101: *The nutrients in Swiss chard, beta carotene, vitamin E and C, zinc, lutein and quercitin, are good for the skin. It also contains vitamin K, which helps keep the brain and nervous system functioning properly.*

Craneberry Tea

We've modernized this traditional Northwestern Native American recipe. First called "crane berries" because of the shape of the plant in blossom, the tangy cranberries mixed with the sweetness of the oranges and the steeped cinnamon make a refreshing drink. We recommend this tea after a meal or even during chemotherapy infusions. It can be served hot or cold. Stores well, covered in the refrigerator, for at least a week.

....

Targeted Side Effects: Fatigue, hydration, nausea

A good source of vitamin C

Calories: 100; Total Fat: 0 g; Saturated Fat: 0 g; Total Carbohydrate: 25 g; Fiber: 1 g; Protein: 0 g

....

Makes 10 servings
Ingredients:

50 ounces water

7 tea bags, black or chamomile

60 ounces 100% cranberry–berry juice

5 cinnamon sticks, broken in half

2 oranges, sliced

Health Tip 101: *Cranberries contain antioxidants and nutrients that help prevent urinary tract infections by inhibiting certain bacteria from sticking to the bladder walls.*

Directions:

1. In a large pot, boil water, add tea bags, and steep for three to five minutes. Remove tea bags.

2. Add cranberry–berry juice and cinnamon sticks.

3. Reduce heat to simmer. Add orange slices and simmer for three minutes.

4. Remove cinnamon sticks (use as a garnish, if desired). Serve hot in mugs.

5. For cold tea, after removing cinnamon sticks, cool tea to room temperature. Add ice cubes to serve immediately or chill in refrigerator until ready to serve.

QUICK GLANCE CHART OF RECIPES WITH TREATMENT PHASES AND TARGETED SIDE EFFECTS

	Pretreatment/Surgery	Radiation	Chemotherapy	Hormone Therapy	Remission/Prevention	Anemia	Blood Sugar Regulation	Bone Health	Chemo Brain
BREAKFAST									
Amaranth with Spices, p. 15		x	x	x	x		x		
Breakfast Vegetable Medley, p. 13	x	x	x	x	x		x		
Cheese Omelet with Veggies and Greens, p. 6	x	x	x	x	x		x		x
Creamy Rice Pudding, p. 4	x	x							
French Toast with Nut Butter, p. 14	x	x			x				x
Grits and Eggs, p. 5	x	x	x	x	x		x		
Oat Scones, p. 8	x	x	x	x	x				
Pear and Almond Muesli, p. 9	x	x	x	x	x		x		
Quinoa and Cinnamon Cereal, p. 10	x	x	x	x	x		x		
Savory Oatmeal, p. 11		x	x	x	x				
Steak and Eggs, p. 12		x	x			x			x
Stewed Fruit, p. 7	x	x	x			x			
LUNCH									
Artichoke, Bean, Hazelnut, and Asparagus Salad, p. 40		x		x	x				x
Bangers and Mash, p. 19		x		x	x				
Bibimbap, p. 37	x	x	x						x
Borscht, p. 18	x	x	x	x	x	x			
Carrot Soup with Fennel, p. 32		x	x	x	x				
Chickpea and Coconut Soup, p. 22		x	x	x					
Cold Eggplant Salad, p. 24	x	x	x						
Dandelion and Arugula Salad, p. 20	x	x		x	x	x			
Eloise's Salmon Patties, p. 35	x	x	x	x	x				x
Fall Bounty Squash Soup, p. 34	x	x	x	x	x				
Frittata with Spinach, Mushrooms, and Onions, p. 29		x	x			x			
Kale Salad, p. 26	x	x		x	x				
Mac and Cheese with Sausage, p. 30		x	x						
Mushroom Buckwheat Soup, p. 23	x	x	x			x			
Mushroom Soup with Onions, p. 31		x	x	x			x		
Pasta with Pesto, p. 28	x	x	x	x	x				
Quinoa Salad, p. 25	x	x	x	x	x		x		
Rice Pasta with Sugar Snap Peas, Peanuts, and Asparagus, p. 27		x		x	x		x		

Constipation	Diarrhea	Fat Metabolism	Fatigue	Gas and Bloating	Hot Flashes/Night Sweats	Hydration	Infection	Insomnia	Joint Pain	Loss of Appetite	Muscle Aches	Nausea	Peripheral Neuropathy	Scarring	Skin and Hair Damage	Wound Healing
			X		X										X	
			X		X											X
			X										X			
	X		X					X				X				
			X													X
			X										X			
			X													
X			X					X								
			X					X				X				
X								X							X	X
			X									X				X
X			X													X
			X		X											
			X		X											X
			X									X				
X			X													
X				X								X				X
			X		X											
			X													X
X										X						
			X		X			X	X							
X																X
			X													X
X					X			X								
			X													
			X													X
			X													
			X				X									
			X					X								
			X		X											

	Pretreatment/Surgery	Radiation	Chemotherapy	Hormone Therapy	Remission/Prevention	Anemia	Blood Sugar Regulation	Bone Health	Chemo Brain
Salad Niçoise, p. 33		x	x	x					
Sesame Noodles with Broccoli and Carrots, p. 36	x	x	x	x	x				
Split Pea Soup, p. 21	x	x	x	x	x				
Stuffed Portobello Mushrooms, p. 38		x			x	x			
DINNER,									
Chicken with Apricots and Chickpeas, p. 62		x	x			x			
Chili Paste Salmon, p. 44	x	x	x	x	x	x	x		
Coconut Fish Curry, p. 48	x	x	x	x	x				x
Cod with Basil Sauce, p. 43	x	x	x	x	x				
Dahl with Spices, p. 52	x	x	x	x	x	x			
Eloise's Creole Gumbo, p. 55		x	x			x			
Eloise's Turkey and Dumplings, p. 56	x	x	x	x	x				
Grilled Halibut with Orange Ginger Sauce, p. 58	x	x	x	x	x				
Hot and Sour Soup with Mushrooms, p. 61	x	x	x	x	x				
Lentil Loaf, p. 49	x	x	x	x	x				
Pasta and Sardines, p. 50		x	x	x					
Seafood Stew, p. 54		x	x	x					
Shrimp Casserole, p. 53		x	x	x					x
Steak and Vegetable Fajitas, p. 46		x	x			x			x
Stuffed Peppers, p. 60	x	x	x	x	x				
Sweet and Sour Baked Chicken, p. 59		x	x						
Turkey Florentine, p. 51		x		x	x			x	
Turkey Meatloaf, p. 45		x	x	x	x	x			
SIDE DISHES									
Baked Garnet Yams with Dried Fruit (Tzimmes), p. 68		x	x		x	x			
Broccoli with Gomasio and Ginger, p. 77		x		x	x				
Brown Rice Festival, p. 67	x	x	x	x	x				
Cabbage Slaw with Almonds and Apples, p. 66		x		x	x			x	
Carrot, Ginger, and Arame Salad, p. 83	x	x	x	x	x				
Chop Chop Salad, p. 80	x	x		x	x			x	
Cucumber, Cantaloupe, and Squash Salad, p. 76		x	x						
Garlic Snow Peas, p. 78	x	x	x	x	x				
Grilled Asparagus, p. 70	x	x	x	x	x				
Grilled Tomatoes, p. 73	x	x	x	x	x				
Mary's Carrot and Raisin Salad, p. 69	x	x	x	x	x	x			
Mashed Root Vegetables with Herbs, p. 75		x	x	x	x			x	

Constipation	Diarrhea	Fat Metabolism	Fatigue	Gas and Bloating	Hot Flashes/Night Sweats	Hydration	Infection	Insomnia	Joint Pain	Loss of Appetite	Muscle Aches	Nausea	Peripheral Neuropathy	Scarring	Skin and Hair Damage	Wound Healing
			x		x						x					
			x		x			x	x							
		x	x		x											
			x													
			x													x
			x	x								x				
x			x						x				x			
			x		x				x							
			x													
x					x				x							
			x					x					x			
			x		x				x							
			x							x						
		x	x													
			x		x											
			x		x				x							x
			x		x								x			
			x										x			
			x													
			x													x
			x					x								
			x					x				x				
										x						x
					x				x		x	x				
x			x													
x					x								x			
x				x								x			x	
			x													
x																x
x			x													
			x													x
			x		x											x
x									x							x
x			x						x							x

	Pretreatment/Surgery	Radiation	Chemotherapy	Hormone Therapy	Remission/Prevention	Anemia	Blood Sugar Regulation	Bone Health	Chemo Brain
Papaya Salad, p. 72	x		x						
Potato Pancakes with Zucchini and Carrots, p. 82		x	x						
Roasted Brussels Sprouts with Garlic Sauce, p. 74	x	x	x	x	x				
Roasted Vegetables, p. 71	x	x	x	x	x		x		
Sweet and Sour Cabbage, p. 79	x	x		x	x		x		
Tomato, Pumpkin Seed, and Cilantro Salad, p. 81	x	x		x	x				
SNACKS									
Banana Protein Shake, p. 96	x	x	x						
Beet Spread with Sour Cream, Dill and Horseradish, p. 90		x	x			x	x		
Blueberry Smoothie, p. 93		x	x		x				
Green Smoothie with Probiotics, p. 95	x			x	x				
Hummus with Turmeric, p. 91		x		x	x		x		
Mushroom and Walnut Pâté, p. 92	x	x	x	x	x	x			
Quick Greens, p. 89	x	x		x	x				
Smoked Salmon with Cream Cheese, p. 88	x	x	x	x	x				
Spicy Roasted Chickpeas, p. 87	x	x	x		x	x			
Trail Mix, p. 86	x	x	x	x	x				
Zucchini and Carrot Muffins, p. 94	x	x	x	x	x		x		
DESSERTS									
Balsamic Blueberries, p. 104			x		x		x		
Banana with Chocolate and Walnuts, p. 100	x	x	x	x	x				
Carob Fudge, p. 101			x		x	x		x	
Chocolate Covered Figs, p. 99			x	x	x	x	x		
Chocolate Pudding, p. 105	x	x	x	x	x				
Crispy Chewies, p. 103	x	x	x	x	x				
Melon "Ice Cream," p. 102	x	x	x						
EATING AS A PRESCRIPTION									
Bone Broth, p. 108		x	x	x		x		x	
Coconut "Ice Cream," p. 114	x	x	x	x	x				
Mango Lassi, p. 112	x	x			x	x			
Nutritional Vegetable Broth, p. 110		x	x	x		x		x	
Nutty Smoothie, p. 113	x	x	x	x	x				
Smothered Liver, p. 109		x	x			x			
Tuna and Avocado Salad, p. 111	x	x	x	x	x				

Constipation	Diarrhea	Fat Metabolism	Fatigue	Gas and Bloating	Hot Flashes/Night Sweats	Hydration	Infection	Insomnia	Joint Pain	Loss of Appetite	Muscle Aches	Nausea	Peripheral Neuropathy	Scarring	Skin and Hair Damage	Wound Healing
X									X		X	X		X		
X			X													
X			X		X											X
			X													
X										X	X	X				
			X		X			X			X					X
		X	X						X							
X			X													
X			X						X							
X					X											
			X					X								
			X													
X			X					X								
			X		X				X							X
			X									X				
			X													
X																
																X
			X													X
										X						
X			X													
			X													
			X													
X			X													
					X			X		X		X				
										X		X				
		X								X		X				X
			X			X	X			X		X				
X			X					X		X		X				
		X								X						
		X	X							X						X

	Pretreatment/Surgery	Radiation	Chemotherapy	Hormone Therapy	Remission/Prevention	Anemia	Blood Sugar Regulation	Bone Health	Chemo Brain
BEVERAGES									
Blueberry Kale Juice, p. 118	x	x	x						
Craneberry Tea, p. 120	x	x	x	x	x				
Jazzy Apple Juice, p. 117	x		x						
Orange-Orange Juice, p. 117	x		x						
Power Green Juice, p. 118	x	x	x	x	x				
Vegetable–Fruit Drink, p. 119		x	x			x			

Constipation	Diarrhea	Fat Metabolism	Fatigue	Gas and Bloating	Hot Flashes/Night Sweats	Hydration	Infection	Insomnia	Joint Pain	Loss of Appetite	Muscle Aches	Nausea	Peripheral Neuropathy	Scarring	Skin and Hair Damage	Wound Healing
			X			X				X						
			X			X						X				
X			X			X										
			X			X										X
			X			X										
			X			X										

Healing is impossible in loneliness; it is the opposite of loneliness. Conviviality is healing. To be healed we must come with all the other creatures to the feast of Creation.

— Wendell Berry

COMMON FOODS AND THEIR NUTRIENT CONTENT

Almonds Per 95 gram serving, almonds contain 12 grams of dietary fiber, 25% dietary calcium, and 20% of RDA dietary iron. They are low in sugar and high in folate, vitamin E, choline, magnesium, phosphorus and manganese. They contain no cholesterol.

Apricots High in fiber and antioxidant carotenoids. Apricots are very high in iron and vitamins A and C. They are anti-inflammatory and have a low glycemic index.

Artichokes Low in saturated fat and cholesterol. They are a good source of niacin, magnesium, manganese, phosphorus, potassium, and copper, as well as dietary fiber. Artichokes also contain vitamins C and K and folate.

Avocados Contain protein, 40% of RDA dietary fiber, and a number of good fats. They are high in vitamin E and are a good source of vitamins C and K and folate.

Basil Provides vitamin A, C, and E and is a good source of riboflavin and niacin. It also supplies vitamins K and B6, folate, calcium, iron, magnesium phosphorus, potassium, zinc, copper, and manganese.

Beef Contains a concentrated amount of protein. It is high in phosphorus and vitamins B12, D, and K.

Beets An excellent source of dietary fiber. They also provide vitamin C, magnesium, potassium, folate, and manganese. This food contains a lot of sugar, so it's best not to overdo it.

Blueberries This fruit has a low glycemic index and is low in saturated fat, cholesterol, and sodium. It is a great source of dietary fiber and a good source of vitamins C and K and the minerals manganese and chromium.

Broccoli   An anti-inflammatory with a low glycemic index. It is also high in fiber, beta carotene, and lutein. Broccoli is particularly high in vitamins K, C, and A. It also contains indole-3-carbinol, which is helpful in decreasing inflammation.

Brussels Sprouts   Contain high amounts of vitamins C, A, and K. One cup contains 4 grams of protein and has a low glycemic index. Brussels sprouts are a good source of thiamine, riboflavin, iron, magnesium, phosphorus, and copper. They are high in dietary fiber and contain a chemical constituent known as indole-3-carbinol that acts to decrease inflammation. Brussels sprouts also contain omega-3 fatty acids.

Butternut Squash   Contains high amounts of vitamins A, C, and K and the mineral manganese. It has a low glycemic index and is low in saturated fat and cholesterol. It provides a good source of vitamins E and B6, thiamine, niacin, folate, calcium, and magnesium. It also contains omega-3 and omega-6 fatty acids.

Cabbage   Contains vitamins A and C, folate, iron, copper, and manganese. It has a low glycemic index and is an excellent source of fiber. It also is a good source of niacin, calcium, and vitamin K.

Cantaloupe   Contains dietary fiber and, surprisingly, has a relatively low glycemic index. It is also a good source of niacin, folate, and vitamins B6, A, C, and K. It contains omega-3 and omega-6 fatty acids.

Cashews   Contain a good amount of iron, magnesium, phosphorus, and copper. They have a low glycemic index and contain both omega-3 and omega-6 fatty acids.

Cauliflower   Cauliflower is high in vitamins C and B6, dietary fiber, folate, and pantothenic acid. It is low in saturated fat and cholesterol and contains omega-3 and omega-6 fatty acids.

Celery   A great source of dietary fiber and vitamins A, C, and K. It also contains good amounts of potassium and manganese and some omega-6 fatty acids.

Chard   High in vitamins A and C and a great source of dietary fiber. It provides thiamine, folate, and zinc and has a very low glycemic index. It contains omega-3 and omega-6 fatty acids.

Cherries   High in vitamin C and dietary fiber. Cherries contain omega-3 and omega-6 fatty acids.

Chickpeas (Garbanzo beans)   Are a rich source of iron and folate. They are low in saturated fat and very low in cholesterol. Chickpeas are a very good source of dietary fiber, protein, and copper, and contain a hefty amount of omega-6 fatty acids.

Chocolate   Low in cholesterol and a good source of iron, copper, manganese, and magnesium. It contains antioxidants and both omega-3 and omega-6 fatty acids.

Cilantro   A good source of thiamine, zinc, and dietary fiber. It also contains vitamins A, C, E, K, and B6, as well as the minerals calcium, iron, magnesium, potassium, copper, and manganese.

Cinnamon   Contains vitamin K and iron, calcium, and manganese.

Coconut Milk   Contains a good amount of iron and vitamin C. It has a low glycemic index and is low in cholesterol. It also is a good source of protein as well as omega-6 fatty acids.

Cod   A good source of lean protein. It is low in saturated fat and provides a good source of vitamins B12 and B6 and the mineral selenium.

Carrots   High in vitamins A and C. It provides a good amount of dietary fiber, thiamine, niacin, folate, and manganese. Carrots also contain both omega-3 and omega-6 fatty acids.

Cranberries   A great source of vitamin C and E. They are a good source of dietary fiber and are low in saturated fat and cholesterol. Cranberries also contain both omega-3 and omega-6 fatty acids.

Cumin   Has a very low glycemic index and is a very good source of iron and calcium. It is also a good source of magnesium and manganese and contains omega-6 and omega-3 fatty acids.

Fennel Root   This root vegetable and spice is a great source of vitamin C and has a very low glycemic index. It is a very good source of dietary fiber as well as calcium, iron, and magnesium.

Figs   Very low in saturated fat and cholesterol and a great source of dietary fiber, vitamin K, calcium, potassium, and iron. Figs also contain protein and omega-6 fatty acids.

Garlic   Low in saturated fat and cholesterol, garlic contains protein and is an excellent source of vitamin C, calcium, and iron. It also provides a good source of vitamin B6 and manganese and contains omega-3 and omega-6 fatty acids.

Honeydew Melon   Contains a high amount of vitamin C. It is low in saturated fat and cholesterol and contains omega-3 and omega-6 fatty acids.

Kale   A good source of dietary fiber with a very low glycemic index. It is a great source of vitamins A, C, K, and B6. It is a good source of calcium, potassium, copper, and manganese. Kale also contains omega-3 and omega-6 fatty acids.

Lentils   High in iron and low in saturated fat, cholesterol, and sodium. They are a good source of protein, phosphorus, and copper and contain omega-3 and omega-6 fatty acids.

Maitake Mushrooms   A good source of dietary fiber, folate, phosphorus, potassium, and zinc. These mushrooms also contain omega-6 fatty acids.

Okra   A good source of dietary fiber, and low in sodium and fat. It is a great source of vitamin C and a good source of vitamins A, K, and B6, folate, calcium, magnesium, and manganese.

Onions   High in vitamin C, low in saturated fat, and a good source of dietary fiber, vitamin B6, folate, potassium, and manganese. It also contains omega-3 and omega-6 fatty acids.

Parsley   A great source of vitamins A and C, iron, calcium, magnesium, potassium, copper, and manganese. Parsley also contains both omega-3 and omega-6 fatty acids.

Pears   Low in saturated fat and cholesterol and a good source of vitamins C and K. Pears are also an excellent source of dietary fiber.

Peppers   Very high in vitamins C and A and a great source of dietary fiber, vitamin K, potassium, and manganese. Peppers are a very good source of vitamins A, C, E, and B6 and folate. They contain both omega-3 and omega-6 fatty acids.

Papaya   An excellent source of vitamins C and A. It is low in saturated fat and cholesterol and a good source of potassium and folate. Papaya contains omega-3 fatty acid.

Pineapple   A great source of vitamin C and dietary fiber. It is low in saturated fat and cholesterol and contains thiamine, vitamin B6, copper, and both omega-3 and omega-6 fatty acids.

Portobello Mushrooms   A good source of protein and the minerals zinc and manganese and vitamin B6, thiamine, folate, niacin and pantothenic acid.

Prunes   Prunes are good source of protein, vitamin A, calcium, and iron. They are very low in saturated fat and sodium. They also provide vitamins B6 and A.

Quinoa   A very good source of protein, iron, and dietary fiber. It is low in cholesterol and saturated fat and contains magnesium, phosphorus, and manganese.

Salmon   High in protein and a good source of riboflavin, pantothenic acid, and phosphorus. This fish also contains vitamins B12 and B6 and selenium and is an excellent source of omega-3 fatty acid.

Sardines   High in calcium, selenium, phosphorus, and iron. They are a good source of niacin, vitamins D and B12 and contain high amounts of omega-3 and omega-6 fatty acids.

Shrimp   A good source of protein and iron and low in saturated fat. It is a good source of niacin, phosphorus, zinc, vitamin B12, and selenium and contains omega-3 and omega-6 fatty acids.

Spinach   A good source of vitamins A and C, niacin, zinc, and dietary fiber. Other nutrients it provides include vitamins E, K, and B6 and the minerals magnesium, phosphorus, potassium, copper, and manganese.

Sqaush   A very good source of vitamins A and C, low in saturated fat and cholesterol. It is a good source of vitamin E, thiamine, niacin, folate, calcium, and magnesium.

Sugar peas   A very good source of vitamins C and A and very low in saturated fat and cholesterol. It is a good source of riboflavin, vitamin B6, pantothenic acid, magnesium, and potassium and contains omega-6 fatty acids.

Sweet Potato   A very good source of vitamins A and C. Sweet potatoes are low in saturated fat and cholesterol and are a good source of vitamin B6 and potassium. They also contain protein and omega-6 fatty acids.

Tahini   Tahini is the butter of sesame seeds. It is a good source of thiamine, copper, manganese, and calcium. It is low in cholesterol and saturated fat and contains omega-3 and omega-6 fatty acids.

Tomato   Very low in saturated fat and cholesterol. It is a good source of vitamins A and C and dietary fiber and contains thiamine, niacin, vitamin B6, folate, and potassium.

Turkey   A very good source of protein and iron. It is also a good source of phosphorus, zinc, and selenium and contains omega-3 and omega-6 fatty acids.

Walnuts Low in cholesterol and a good source of copper, manganese, and iron. These nuts are a very good source of omega-3 and omega-6 fatty acids.

Zucchini High in vitamin C. It is a good source of riboflavin, vitamin B6, manganese, and dietary fiber.

The world is so empty if one thinks only of mountains, rivers, and cities; but to know someone who thinks and feels with us, and who, though distant, is close to us in spirit, this makes the earth for us an inhabited garden.

—Johann Wolfgang von Goethe

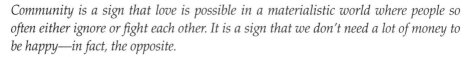

Community is a sign that love is possible in a materialistic world where people so often either ignore or fight each other. It is a sign that we don't need a lot of money to be happy—in fact, the opposite.

—Jean Vanier, Community and Growth

CANCER SUPPORT RESOURCES

American Association for Cancer Research
www.aacr.org

The mission of the American Association for Cancer Research is to prevent and cure cancer through research, education, communication, and collaboration.

American Cancer Society
www.cancer.org
1-800-227-2345
1875 Connecticut Ave., NW Suite 730
Washington, DC 20009
The American Cancer Society is the nationwide, community-based, voluntary health organization dedicated to eliminating cancer as a major health problem by preventing cancer, saving lives, and diminishing suffering from cancer through research, education, advocacy, and service.

American Lung Association
www.lungusa.org
1-800-586-4872
1301 Pennsylvania Ave., NW
Washington, DC 20004
Their mission is to save lives by improving lung health and preventing lung disease.

The Breast Cancer Action
www.breastcancerfund.org
1-866-760-8223
1388 Sutter St., Suite 400

San Francisco, CA 94109
The Breast Cancer Action carries the voices of people affected by breast cancer to inspire and compel the changes necessary to end the breast cancer epidemic.

Cancer Lifeline
www.cancerlifeline.org
206-297-2500
1-800-255-5505
Provides emotional support, resources, educational classes, and exercise programs designed to support people in all stages of the cancer process. They welcome patients, survivors, and their families, friends, co-workers, and caregivers.

Cancer Really Sucks
www.cancerreallysucks.org
1-319-393-9681
P.O. Box 11264
Cedar Rapids, IA 52410-1264
A website designed for teens looking for hope and ways to cope with cancer in their world.

Cancer Resources of Mendocino County
www.crcmendocino.org
707-937-3833
Its mission is to improve the quality of life for those in Mendocino County faced with cancer.

Colon Cancer Alliance
www.ccalliance.org
1-877-422-2030
1025 Vermont Ave., NW, Suite 1066
Washington, DC 20005
Colon Cancer Alliance's mission is to knock colon cancer out of the top three cancer killers list. We are doing this by championing prevention, funding cutting-edge research, and providing the highest quality patient support services.

Corporate Angel Network
www.corpangelnetwork.org
Westchester County Airport
One Loop Road

White Plains, NY 10604-1215
The Corporate Angel Network is the only charitable organization in the United States whose sole mission is to help cancer patients access the best possible treatment for their specific type of cancer by arranging free travel to treatment across the country using empty seats on corporate jets.

Foundation for Women's Cancer
www.foundationforwomenscancer.org
1-312-578-1439
230 West Monroe, Suite 2528
Chicago, IL 60606
The foundation's mission is to facilitate synergy between organizations who share the goals of gynecologic cancer prevention, early detection, and optimal care of women living with these malignancies.

Intercultural Cancer Council
http://icsnetwork.org
1-713-798-4617
Baylor College of Medicine
1709 Dryden Road, Suite 1025
Houston, TX 77030-3411
Intercultural Cancer Council promotes policies, programs, partnerships, and research to eliminate the unequal burden of cancer among racial and ethnic minorities and medically underserved patients in the United States and its associate territories.

Mothers and Daughters
www.mothersdaughters.org
1-410-778-1982
The organization provides free support services designed to help mothers who have daughters battling breast cancer.

Multiple Myeloma Research Foundation
www.multiplemyeloma.org
1-203-972-1250
383 Main Ave., 5th Floor
Norwalk, CT 06851
The MMRF relentlessly pursues innovative means that accelerate the development of next-generation multiple myeloma treatments to extend the lives of patients and lead to a cure.

National Cancer Institute

www.cancer.gov

The NCI coordinates the National Cancer Program, which conducts and supports research, training, health information dissemination, and other programs to the cause of diagnosis, prevention, and treatment of cancer, rehabilitation from cancer, and the continuing care of the cancer patients and their families.

National Ovarian Cancer Coalition

www.ovarian.org

1-888-682-7426
500 NE Spanish River Blvd., Suite 8
Boca Raton, FL 33431
The mission of the organization is to save lives by fighting tirelessly to prevent and cure ovarian cancer and to improve the quality of life for survivors.

Northwest Hope and Healing

www.nwhopeandhealing.org

206-615-2888
P.O. Box 16069
Seattle WA 98116
Northwest Hope and Healing offers financial support to women in need who are battling breast and gynecological cancers in the Seattle, Washington, area.

Patient Advocate Foundation

www.patientadvocate.org

1-800-532-5274
700 Thimble Shoals Blvd., Suite 200
Newport News, VA 23606
Patient Advocate Foundation provides patient case management services to Americans with chronic, life-threatening, and debilitating illnesses.

Prevent Cancer Foundation

www.preventcancer.org

1600 Duke St.
Alexandria, VA 22314
The Foundation's mission is to save lives through cancer prevention and early detection.

BIBLIOGRAPHY

Boeing, Heiner et al. "Critical Review: Vegetables and Fruit in the Prevention of Chronic Diseases." *European Journal of Nutrition* 51(2012): 637–63.

Cambell, T. Colin and Thomas M. Cambell II. *The China Study*. Dallas, TX: BenBella Books, 2005.

Dehal, Ahmed et al. "Impact of Diabetes Mellitus and Insulin Use on Survival After Colorectal Cancer Diagnosis: The Cancer Prevention Study – II Nutrition Cohort." *Journal of Clinical Oncology* 30(2011): 53–9.

Demers, Mimi et al. "A Randomized Double-Blind Controlled Trial: Impact of Probiotics on Diarrhea in Patients Treated with Pelvic Radiation." *Clinical Nutrition* 24(2013).

Doyle, Coleen et al. "Nutrition and Physical Activity During and After Cancer Treatment: An American Cancer Society Guide for Informed Choices." *CA: A Cancer Journal for Clinicians* 56(2006): 323–53.

European Prospective Investigation into Cancer and Nutrition Project. "EPIC Study." accessed August 12, 2014, http://epic.iarc.fr

James-Martin, Genevieve et al. "Information Needs of Cancer Patients and Survivors Regarding Diet, Exercise and Weight Management: A Qualitative Study." *European Journal of Cancer Care* 23(2013): 340–48.

Kiss, Nicole K. et al. "The Effect of Nutrition Intervention in Lung Cancer Patients Undergoing Chemotherapy and/or Radiotherapy: A Systemic Review." *Nutrition and Cancer* 66(2013): 47–56.

Kushi, Lawrence H. "American Cancer Society Guidelines on Nutrition and Physical Activity for Cancer Prevention: Reducing the Risk of Cancer with Healthy Food Choices and Physical Activity." *CA: A Cancer Journal for Clinicians* 62(2012): 30–67.

Marin Caro, Maria M. et al. "Nutritional Intervention and Quality of Life in Adult Oncology Patients." *Clinical Nutrition* 26(2007): 289–301.

Mobashori, Ali et al. "Osteogenic Effects of Resveratrol in vitro: Potential for the Prevention and Treatment of Osteoporosis." *Annual of the New York Academy of Sciences* 1290(2013): 59–66.

National Cancer Institute. "Fact Sheets: Diet and Nutrition." accessed August 12, 2014, http://www.cancer.gov/cancertopics/factsheet/diet

Nicastro, Humberto et al. "An Overview of the Therapeutic Effects of Leucine Supplementation on Skeletal Muscle Under Atrophic Conditions." *Amino Acids* 40(2011): 287–300.

Ravasco, Paula et al. "Does Nutrition Influence Quality of Life in Cancer Patients Undergoing Radiotherapy?" *Radiotherapy and Oncology* 67(2003): 215–20.

Ravasco, Paula et al. "Dietary Counseling Improves Patient Outcomes: A Prospective, Randomized, Controlled Trial in Colorectal Cancer Patients Undergoing Radiotherapy." *Journal of Clinical Oncology* 23(2005): 1431–38.

Self. "Nutrition Data." accessed August 12, 2014, http://nutritiondata .self.com

Strassser, Florian et al. "Prevention of Docetaxel- or Paclitaxel- Associated Taste Alterations in Cancer Patients with Oral Glutamine: A Randomized, Placebo-Controlled, Double-Blind Study." *Oncologist* 13(2008):337–46.

Tete Stefano et al. "Nutrition and Cancer Prevention." *International Journal of Immunopathology and Pharmacology* 25(2012): 573–81.

Wolf, Sherry et al. "Chemotherapy-Induced Peripheral Neuropathy: Prevention and Treatment Strategies." *European Journal of Cancer* 44(2008): 1507–15.

ACKNOWLEDGMENTS

No one is an island, untouched by experiences, assistance, or the luck of circumstance. The genius occurs at the nexus where they happen to meet. I would like to express my sincere gratitude to the technical advice and mentorship that I have received from many people, particularly Jill Marsal and Julia Pastore, as well as Mary Travers, Lisa Konick, Renae Stott Wilbur, and all my teachers along the way. Thank you Stewart and Nancy Hopkins for the grace and beauty you've added to our book.

I'd like to express my sincere love and thanks to my family and friends who have given me time to think and work and have encouraged me wholeheartedly. You've provided the fuel necessary to believe in the fruition of this book. Thank you Mary, Jimmie, and Kevin Price, Eloise Wilson, Cypress and Nia Price-Nascimento, and Glen Gallagher. I'd like to thank my co-author for being game and jumping aboard this faithful ride.

Finally, I'd like to thank my patients for being my greatest teachers and inspiration. You fight the good fight every day, and I hope this book can make your life easier.

—*Lisa A. Price*

I'd like to thank my co-author for her sensitivity and kindness in understanding the need for this book and choosing me to be part of the project; Jill Marshal and Julia Pastore for guiding me through learning the new language of writing a book; Bastyr University for providing me with information that underlies my firmest belief that food is medicine and can work miracles in people's lives; and Elliot Bay Books in Seattle, where my co-author and I held all our face to face meetings.

Thanks to Megan Gordon, cookbook author, for her generous advice. A prayer "shout out" to Ann Miller whose advice launched me into my career in nutrition, and to Stewart Hopkins and Nancy Werner, whose talent and friendship completed the picture.

—*Susan Gins*

Index

About the Authors

DR. LISA A. PRICE, ND, is a licensed naturopathic physician in the State of Washington (1999–current), a National Institutes of Health Research Fellow (2005–2010), and an adjunct faculty member at Bastyr University. She teaches biochemistry to Masters of Science candidates in Nutrition. Her classes focus on the physiological effects of nutrients as well as the standard biochemistry concepts.

As an NIH research fellow, she investigated the immunological effects of a medicinal mushroom in normal immune systems as well as in women with breast cancer. Her research included both clinical and basic science study. She has published peer-reviewed scientific papers and abstracts, has written many articles on health and nutrition, and has presented her findings at scientific conferences (American Society of Pharmacology). She produced and edited an online newsletter, *Sound Integrated Health News*, in the mid-2000s.

She has a Bachelor of Science degree in biochemistry and microbiology, and completed her Master of Science graduate work in biochemistry at the State University of New York, Syracuse. Prior to becoming a naturopathic physician, she worked professionally as a research scientist. In 2011, she was asked to join a complementary cancer care specialty practice where she currently works in conjunction and collaboration with medical oncologists and radiologists in major conventional cancer centers in Washington. As an alternative provider, she prescribes therapies that help to decrease side effects of the conventional therapies and attempt to improve quality of life for these patients via supplements, diet, and exercise all while staying out of the way of conventional medicines. She has a reputation with her patients of using dietary means to control, decrease, or mitigate side effects.

Dr. Price was asked to join a news media group in April 2013. Dr. James Gore, director of Ariel Productions (KKNW, 1150 AM, Seattle, WA), sought an alternative practitioner for a health segment. She produces a show once a month with this group. In addition, she does several public lectures each year, including several for cancer support organizations.

SUSAN GINS, MA, MS, CN, voted "Best Nutritionist in Seattle" by City Search, is a Washington State Department of Health Certified Nutritionist. Started in 1998, Gins continues a private nutrition practice, Nourish, in Seattle and Issaquah, WA, where she counsels patients with myriad diseases and health concerns.

Gins has given lectures and cooking classes for Cancer LifeLine, The Port of Seattle, Seattle Housing Authority, Starbucks Coffee, Adobe Systems, and Fenwick & West, LLC, among others. Hired by the Muckleshoot Tribal School K-12, she successfully created and initiated nutrition programs for the lunch program, including starting a salad bar, introducing non-white grains, serving soy milk for the lactose intolerant, and bringing back traditional tribal foods for the children.

Gins appeared several times on KUOW, an NPR local station, and KCPQ, a local TV channel. She produced two DVDs: *ETC: Eating, Teens and Calcium* on nondairy sources for lactose intolerant teens, and *All About Menopause: Natural Alternatives to Hormone Replacement Therapy*. Prior to becoming a nutritionist, Gins, who also has a Master's of Arts in textiles, had a successful custom weaving studio, *That's Art!*

For more recipes and information, visit www.cookingthroughcancer.com

About the Photographer

STEWART HOPKINS is a professional photographer based in the Pacific Northwest. His work appears in *Weekends For Two In The Pacific Northwest*, a guide to bed and breakfasts, *The Fountain and the Mountain*, an architectural history of the University of Washington, and *The University of Washington Experience*, a guide to student life on campus. He is dedicated to using photography to improve people's lives.

www.stewarthopkins.com